MASTERS of FASHION

THE LEADING FIGURES BEHIND THE DREAM

Maria Luisa Tagariello

MASTERS
of FASHION

THE LEADING FIGURES BEHIND THE DREAM

Maria Luisa Tagariello

WHITE STAR PUBLISHERS

edited by
VALERIA MANFERTO DE FABIANIS

text
MARIA LUISA TAGARIELLO

graphic design
CLARA ZANOTTI

editorial staff GIADA FRANCIA / GIORGIA RAINERI

5 A 1963 portrait of Audrey Hepburn in a suit designed by Givenchy.

Contents

6 After Lee Alexander McQueen's death, Sarah Burton took over the creative directorship of the House. The 2011-2012 Fall/Winter collection, entitled "The Ice Queen and her Court," shows how she shared the master's vision.

The leading figures behind the dream

"FORTUNE ALWAYS COMES TO THE ASSISTANCE OF
HE WHO STRONGLY DESIRES SOMETHING," WROTE
CHRISTIAN DIOR IN HIS MEMOIRS.

Fortune, destiny, or providence – Dior would have us believe that the lives of those designers who have made fashion history are driven by outside influences. And in this sense, many of them did concoct their own personal superstitions: from Dior's lily-of-the-valley charm sewn into the seams of garments and stowed away in the breast pocket of his own jacket, to Coco Chanel's number 5, hidden in the chandelier at Rue Cambon and later the name of her famous perfume; from the "S" of Schiaparelli and Shocking to Jean-Paul Gaultier's fetishistic striped t-shirt. However, such cases could also be indicative of a vocation. A vocation so strong that it forces one into submission. So then, it is a matter of lives that follow destiny—destined to create, to make dreams come true, to enter history, because they are intertwined with history, and constitute an important chapter of it.

A vocation that in many cases was revealed in childhood. As in that of Jean-Paul Gaultier, who made clothes for his stuffed animals and created bracelets out of old tin cans. Such too was the case of Valentino Garavani, who, as a child created his first dress for his aunt Rosa, the owner of a shop that sold trimmings in Voghera, where he used to spend his afternoons playing with fabric remnants. For others it was a matter of an uncontrollable creative streak, a keen sensibility, destined to channel itself towards fashion at a more mature age.

When little more than a child, Elsa Schiaparelli was composing passionate poems; as an adult, she invented fantasies, prints, silhouettes and extraordinary hats with the help of her artist friends. Christian Dior made drawings for the pages of *Le Figaro Illustré*, and opened an art gallery, before launching the "New Look." In the case of others, life initially seemed to indicate a different course, but was, later, redirected towards its true destiny. This is what happened to Vivienne Westwood, a provincial schoolteacher in England, who became costume designer for the Sex Pistols. And to Gianfranco Ferré, who went from architect to an "architect of fashion." And, again, to Emilio Pucci, Marquis of Barsento, a ski champion and Second World War pilot, who nonetheless entered history as "Prince of Prints."

One might ask what would have happened had they taken other routes. Had Coco Chanel been less tenacious and courageous in confronting the adversity that life had in store for her; had Vivienne Westwood not met Malcolm McLaren; had Christian Dior not paid heed to those portents that led him to found his House at the age of forty; had Jean-Paul Gaultier not knocked so insistently on

Pierre Cardin's door, had Gianni Versace never abandoned his mother's shop—she had been a seamstress at No. 13 via Tommaso Gulli in Reggio Calabria—in order to seek his fortune in Milan.

Certain milestones in fashion history would not exist today. Neither Valentino red, nor the woman's tuxedo, neither greige, nor the matelassé purse nor the *Little Black Dress*. Indeed, not even fashion as we know it today would exist because these creative minds became the interpreters of their own times; they understood how to embrace political and social change; they were creators of not only beautiful garments but of fashion intended to express *Zeitgeist*: the kind that kindles desire, activates million-dollar deals, but above all decodes the spirit of the times.

"Fashion is not an art but it needs an artist to exist. Clothing is certainly less important than music, architecture, painting, but it was what I knew how to do and did do, participating in the transformations of my era." In those words by Yves Saint Laurent, spoken on the occasion of his farewell show, in January 2002, lies the full meaning of a fashion understood as an expression of a specific and, simultaneously, a collective personality.

From women's liberation, as achieved by Coco Chanel, to the YSL label tuxedo that replaced the evening gown and became the symbol of female emancipation in 1966, to the 1980s of Armani, creator of the wardrobe of the powerful and sensually androgynous career woman, all the way to the refined poverty of Yohji Yamamoto and the intellectual fashion of Miuccia Prada. From haute couture to prêt-à-porter, from the beginning of the last century to today, the creations in "Masters of Fashion" convey the sense of a position that is not only aesthetic but also social, often even political. If clothes are the fabric of history, the weft of time, as the journalist Jay Cocks wrote in 1982 about Giorgio Armani, designers are the interpreters of their own era. They bring art, culture, exoticism, even new technologies to the runway. Creative geniuses and visionaries who, through their shows and collections, propagate their own wondrous views of the world. Therefore, the histories of the designers recounted in this book almost have the quality of fairy tales, some lasting a mere blink of an eye and yet so powerful that they will enter history, others are legends already. Couturiers, creators, or as they are more often called today, designers. Veritable artists. Masters. Actors in a dream that is destined to be everlasting.

Coco
CHANEL

"THE MOST DIFFICULT PART OF MY WORK IS ALLOWING THE WOMAN TO FEEL FREE.
NOT MAKING HER WEAR A MASK. NOT MAKING HER MODIFY HER MANNER OF BEING
ACCORDING TO THE CLOTHING SHE WEARS."

AN ORPHAN WITH A STRONG AND ADVENTUROUS CHARACTER.
A YOUNG, AMBITIOUS CABARET SINGER.
A SEAMSTRESS WHO LIBERATED WOMEN FROM CONSTRAINTS,
AND INVENTED FASHION AS WE KNOW IT TODAY.

An independent spirit with a sharp tongue. A lover of famous men. A severe and solitary woman, ruling an empire. Coco Gabrielle Bonheur Chanel was all these women and more. Today, she is a myth, a legend, an icon—a designer who changed the very course of fashion, spurring it onwards into the modern era.

"The toughest part of my job is allowing the woman to feel free. Not making her wear a mask. Not making her modify her way of existence in conformance to the clothing she wears." Practical logic was the principal motive behind all of Coco Chanel's work. With her, for the first time, fashion adjusted itself to the actual demands of the modern woman, one who, like Chanel herself, worked and was constantly active. ("Until this moment we have been dressing useless, idle women, women whose maids helped them get into sleeves; now, instead, we have a clientele of active women; an active woman needs to feel at ease in her own clothes. She needs to be able to roll up her sleeves.")

It was thus that her androgynous, comfortable, and sporty fashion was born, that the iconic hats and accessories, the milestones of fashion history, came to life. Like the *Little Black Jacket*, inspired by a man's jacket, which became a symbol of femininity, and the 2.55 Bag, invented to free hands.

Born on August 19, 1883, in a village in the south of France, Gabrielle Chanel lost her mother at the age of twelve. Her father, a traveling salesman, abandoned his five children. Gabrielle, and her two sisters, grew up within the walls of a convent, the Convent of Aubazine. Seven years spent in this ascetic world instilled in her a sense of austerity and a love for white and black. After leaving the orphanage, Gabrielle sewed during the day and performed, for cavalry officers, in a *café chantant* at night. It seems that her nickname originated here, borrowed from the catchy titles of her repertory: "Qui qu'a vu Coco dans l'Trocadéro?" and "Ko Ri Ko."

An encounter with Étienne Balsan, former officer and polo player, and a key figure in the Parisian *beau monde*, marked a turning point in young Coco's life. It was Étienne, involved in a relationship with the seamstress who was destined to become one of the great entrepreneurs of fashion history, who offered her premises for her first shop, and, more importantly, introduced her to his circle of influential friends. Coco had an exuberant personality. Refusing to ride around like an Amazon, she stole slacks from men's closets and wore striped 'Breton' jerseys and brimless hats, stripped of all ornament to make them simpler and more chic.

In the eyes of women, back then, who were still dressing in long draping garments stuffed with petticoats and corsets, Coco's manner of dressing, was, in truth, somewhat eccentric. Nevertheless, fascinated by her originality, all the high-society women in Paris coveted the hats and creations that Chanel paraded along the Hippodrome de Longchamp.

12 Coco Chanel, in her atelier, surrounded by sketches.

13 Model Anne St. Marie, dressed in a leopard jacket and tube skirt, with Paris in the background.

OF HERSELF, AT AGE SIXTEEN, SHE REMARKED: "MY ALLURE ALREADY BACK
THEN CONSISTED IN THE FACT THAT I DID NOT LOOK LIKE ANYBODY ELSE BECAUSE,
WITHOUT WISHING TO, I ALWAYS DIFFERED FROM EVERYBODY.

This allure, this distinction, induced many women to wish to resemble me and gave all of them a similar look, while my continuously innovative imagination left me alone exceptional. This was an era when it was necessary to be Chanel. A Chanel outfit— rather, the Chanel outfit— seemed to have the power of a talisman that could unquestionably govern fate."

Another man, the most important one, came to play a part in influencing Gabrielle's life, and success. This was Boy Capel, a wealthy English businessman, who financed the opening of her first boutiques in Paris, Deauville, and Biarritz. It was during this period that Chanel transformed the female silhouette. She loosened the tight waist, eliminated the corset, shortened the skirt, and began using jersey—a versatile and inexpensive textile, for which she obtained exclusive rights in 1916. She also made a boy's haircut, and bronzed skin, a hit (allegedly she used to sunbathe entirely in the nude, except for gloved hands). Her style was laid-back, consisting of a straight skirt, cardigan, and soft blouse. Chanel brought an end to an era, and hurled fashion into the next century.

Mademoiselle opened her house of fashion in 1918, at No. 31, Rue Cambon. The young girl from the countryside of Auvergne had become queen of Paris.

The story with Boy (it was to him that Karl Lagerfeld, the brand's artistic director since 1984, dedicated the cult handbag of the same name) was cut short by a dramatic car crash in which Coco's great love lost his life. Ravaged by grief, she sought distraction in Venice with her friend Misia Sert, wife of the artist Josep Maria Sert. It was Misia, Marcel Proust's muse, and model for many great artists of the time, who helped her discover Italy, Russian ballet, and a love for art. Gabrielle knew, and became close friends with, Pablo Picasso, Sergei Diaghilev, and Maurice Ravel, designed costumes for Jean Cocteau's productions (and helped him detox), and hosted Igor Stravinsky and his family, then in significant financial distress, and subsequently became his lover.

Other men entered her life, influenced her career, and became sources of inspiration for new "inventions." Thanks to the young Grand Duke Dmitri Pavlovich of Russia, she met Ernest Beaux, the late Czar's perfumier, and created her first legendary perfume in 1921: Nº5. Two drops on a nude Marilyn Monroe proved it to be the most sensual of all fragrances. Thanks to the Duke of Westminster, the richest man in England, who invited her to his castles and yachts, Coco discovered tweed, drew inspiration from his jackets, his sweaters, the vests worn by his servants and the berets worn by his yacht crews.

"I will dress women in black!" Chanel decided one day—a color that, until then, had been reserved for domestic help, and mourning. The anecdote about the meeting between Paul Poiret and a Coco Chanel dressed in black, has become proverbial. To the celebrated Parisian tailor's query "Why are you dressed in mourning, young lady?" Coco responded: "Because of you, Sir." In the mid-1920s came the *Little Black Dress*, destined to become the most indispensable item of a woman's wardrobe. Whimsical jewels arrived at this time too: pearls, chains, crystals: costume-jewelry creations with which Chanel adorned hats of a severe and essential cut.

15 left A 1954 model of a strapless evening gown adorned with roses, the year that marked the return of Chanel after her withdrawal from the scene and her move from France to Switzerland.

15 right A portrait of Coco by the illustrator Junie Bro Jorgensen. Today, Chanel has become a veritable icon and has entered the halls of pop culture.

Mademoiselle was 55 years old, and at the peak of her success, at the outbreak of the Second World War. She closed her atelier and fled to Switzerland. The only Chanel boutique to remain open during the war era was the perfume shop, outside which, it is said, American soldiers lined up to buy bottles of N°5. During her absence from the Paris fashion scene, Christian Dior came up with the 'New Look,' a return to the sumptuousness of the past, Belle Époque corsets, and layers upon layers of luxury fabrics. Referring to Dior, Chanel observed: "He decks out idlers, he does not dress women; elegance means reducing everything to the most chic, costly, and refined poverty." At 70, she still had a lot to say to the world. Summoning her former collaborators, she reopened her house of fashion.

On February 5, 1954, Chanel chose her magic number as the date for her great return to the runway. Hidden at the top of the famous staircase, at No. 31, Rue Cambon, the designer looked on, in glacial silence, as the models filed by, and, as we may imagine, tried to decipher the faces of the attending reporters. The French press tore her collection to shreds. The return of Chanel was a total fiasco. Across the Atlantic, on the other hand, the reaction was exactly the opposite. As stated in *Life*, "At 71, Gabrielle Chanel proposed more a revolution than a fashion." It was thanks to the American market that Chanel regained all her influence, as she relaunched her style layer upon layer.

Then came the pant suit—with a jacket flowing down gracefully, thanks to a chain sewn into its lining, flat pockets, and jeweled buttons depicting lions (Leo was her sign of the zodiac), camellias (her favorite flower), or double-Cs (the House logo)—adored by Marlene Dietrich, Romy Schneider, Grace Kelly, Brigitte Bardot, Ingrid Bergman, and Elizabeth Taylor. Enter the low-cut two-tone—beige with a black toe—slingback shoe and the matelassé handbag with the chain shoulder-strap.

In the final years of her life, Chanel devoted herself tirelessly to work. At the Hotel Ritz, where she resided, the hotel's concierge would call her studio to report her imminent arrival, as soon as he saw her departing each morning, whereupon an employee would spray the staircase with Chanel N°5. Coco Chanel died, in her hotel room, on January 10, 1971, at the age of 88. "Look, this is the way to die," was the final quip she left to history.

"FASHION FADES, STYLE REMAINS THE SAME"—SO GOES ONE OF COCO CHANEL'S MOST FAMOUS LINES. AND CHANEL INVENTED A STYLE. NOT AN EPHEMERAL AND FLEETING FAD, BUT AN ETERNAL STYLE.

17 Chanel was 71 by the time she returned to the scene, after the interruption caused by the Second World War. It was a period that saw the birth of the suit, with perfectly draped jacket, flat pockets, and bejeweled buttons, an icon revisited over the years and still produced today, in multiple variations, by Karl Lagerfeld.

18 The suit revisited, in 1965, in powder-pink crepe and a mesh of gold sequins.

19 French actress and model Marie-Hélène Arnaud, who gained everlasting fame in 1959, wears a black suit with a white blouse.

Elsa
SCHIAPARELLI

"A STROKE OF COLOR APPEARED BEFORE MY EYES: 'BRILLIANT, IMPOSSIBLE, IMPUDENT, PLEASING AND FULL OF ENERGY.' A SHOCKING COLOR, PURE AND UNDILUTED."

WHO KNOWS WHETHER ELSA SCHIAPARELLI WOULD HAVE BEEN HAPPY TO SEE A BESPECTACLED MARCO ZANINI, WITH TATTOOS AND LONG SIDEBURNS, LOOMING TALL AND GANGLY IN HER WHITE AND LUMINOUS SALON AT NO. 21, PLACE VENDÔME.

Certainly she, the most cultured and eccentric of last century's fashion designers, was accustomed to unexpected encounters. As she recalled in her autobiography (published in Italy as *Shocking Life*, 1954), "unexpected things were always happening on Place Vendôme. One never knew whether it was high or low tide, and who one might meet in the salon on the floor above."

"Female pilots, hostesses, women coming from art schools, from the army or the navy; American mothers travelling, tourists with fake jewels on their hats, aristocrats of the past or present; wives of past, present, or future presidents; ambassadors, actresses, painters, architects, comedians, admirals, generals, reporters, explorers, rulers of all nations, decorators, duchesses and future duchesses, Italian princesses..." crammed together in the atelier on Place Vendôme in the 1930s and 1940s in order to buy Elsa Schiaparelli's clothes and accessories. Today, the address is the label's head office, relaunched by Diego Della Valle, who, in 2005, obtained the rights and archives of the firm, with the idea of "bringing the dream back to life."

It fell to Marco Zanini to revive the legendary brand. Acclaimed by the press as an "excellent debut" and "shocking return," the rise of the 42-year-old designer, formerly at the helm of Rochas, began with his January 2014 debut, during Paris Couture Week. We have no reason to doubt that Schiaparelli would have regarded the show with kindly eyes. Nor, do we believe, would she have criticized the work of the one who wanted to dust off her name—iconic and legendary, yes, but sixty years since the House closed, and became largely forgotten.

Born in Rome on September 10, 1890, to a noblewoman and a father who was a famous arabist, Elsa seemed predestined for an extraordinary life. As a child, bent on growing a magic garden on her own face, she filled her mouth, nose, and ears with seeds. This first attempt to become if not beautiful then at least unique, ended with the intervention of a physician who saved her from death by suffocation. As an adult, she used her creations to render women, who like her, were artists, intellectuals, and unconventionally beautiful, unique.

A book of sensual poetry that she published, as an adolescent, unsettled her family enough to have her enrolled in a Swiss boarding school. A hunger strike convinced her parents to transfer her to London, where she met Count William de Wendt de Kerlor, whom she married in 1914. The couple moved to New York in 1919, where Elsa gave birth to Maria Luisa Yvonne Radha, known as Gogo, her only, and much beloved, daughter. After squandering his wife's modest dowry, however, the Count abandoned her to pursue American dancer Isadora Duncan. Three years later, alone and penniless, she followed her friend Gabrielle, wife of artist Francis Picabia, to Paris, where she established her first studio.

22 Elsa Schiaparelli, in 1951, testing some hats on one of her models.

23 A model in one of the dresses chosen by Wallis Simpson for the occasion of her marriage to the Duke of Windsor, in 1937.

During the inter-war period, Paris was in full creative swing. Art and fashion lived a life of reciprocal exchange. Elsa enjoyed a friendly rapport and collaboration with Jean Cocteau, Cecil Beaton, Man Ray, and above all, Salvador Dalí. The Surrealist painter was an habitué of Schiaparelli's atelier. Together, they created the famous Aragosta look, the hat-like shoe with a pink, velvet, heel in the shape of a lamb chop, with a white frill covering the bone, and the overcoat, a writing desk with drawer-like pockets—bizarre creations that led them to becoming famous for their eccentricity. Yet, in spite of this eccentricity, or perhaps because of it, Elsa won over the Parisian jet set. The most *à la mode* places in the *City of Light* were full of women wearing black-and-white pullovers with *trompe l'oeil* bows—her first sensational creation—hand-knitted by a countrywoman from Armenia. Schiaparelli became a symbol of a sophisticated and intellectual world. "Surrealist" ladies, such as Gala Dalí, the wife of painter Salvador Dalí, Nusch Éluard, the wife of poet Paul Éluard, Marie-Laure de Noailles, aristocratic backer of the art movement, wore her black gloves, with painted pink nails, evening boleros with embroideries based on Jean Cocteau's drawings, evening gowns with images of skeletons, conforming to their wearers ribs, which had the effect of X-rays, swimsuits emblazoned with wriggling fish, and pullovers with pierced hearts and serpents, inspired by sailors' tattoos.

For the eccentric and visionary Schiaparelli, inspiration was everywhere. At the fish market in Copenhagen, she saw women wearing hats made of sheets of folded newspapers; when she returned to Paris she had a fabric printed up with the objects that reminded her of these, and used it for blouses, shoes, hats, and beach items. She created fantastic buttons from the most incredible objects and instituted the use of colored zippers. She accessorized her outfits with enamel necklaces, Plexiglas earrings, and bracelets. She invented rubber culottes for tennis players, designed turbans, embroidered shirts, pompom hats, and combined sports with formal attire, all before anyone else dared to do so.

In 1936, she launched a perfume in the famous bottle that assumed the form of a woman's silhouette. Obligated to give it a name, and to select the color of its packaging, she invented "shocking," a shade of pink that was "brilliant, impossible, impudent, pleasing and full of energy." In her honor, Dalí dyed an enormous, embalmed bear, with drawers in its stomach, in shocking pink dye; Elsa exhibited it in her Schiaparelli salon on the Place Vendôme, which she had opened two years earlier.

Every year, Elsa came up with new collections. Each of these had a theme, which Elsa presented in "modern" shows, with music, and tall, skinny models. "There was the pagan collection, in which women seemed to emerge from a Botticelli painting, wearing garlands and delicate petals of flowers embroidered on simple, classical, clinging skirts. An astrological collection with signs of the Zodiac, stars, a moon and sun that sparkled everywhere. The gaudiest and most brazen of these was the circus, in which clowns, elephants, and horses were covered in fabrics printed with the words "*attention à la peinture*," and which included balloons serving as purses, spats as gloves, ice cream cones as hats, as well as trained dogs and impish monkeys." In 1940, Elsa Schiaparelli went to New York, where she remained until the end of the Second World War. By the time she came back, fashion had changed, Christian Dior's New Look was all the rage. Maison Schiaparelli entered a period of economic decline which led to its closure in 1954. Elsa Schiaparelli died in 1973, bequeathing an inestimable legacy to the history of art and fashion. A dream that has been revived today, in a world that has changed much since then, but which Marco Zanini observes from the same window at No. 21, Place Vendôme.

25 A black, long-sleeved dress with a large pink bow, from 1947, with contrasting embroidery on its back.

26 The famous "Lobster Dress" born of the collaboration between Elsa Schiaparelli and her friend Salvador Dalí. It was the artist who painted a large lobster on the skirt of the white, silk evening gown.

27 A bridal veil finely embroidered with tiny blue seed pearls on display at the Philadelphia Museum of Art exhibition "Shocking! The Art and Fashion of Elsa Schiaparelli," a retrospective dedicated to a veritable fashion icon

Cristóbal

BALENCIAGA

"NO TAILOR CAN MAKE A WOMAN ELEGANT IF SHE ISN'T NATURALLY SO."

FOR MOST PEOPLE, "A BALENCIAGA" IS A GUTSY BAG,
INSPIRED BY THE WORLD OF MOTORCYCLES, AND ONE THAT EVERY WOMAN COVETS.

A cult object that has entered the collective imagination, a global icon, sold in its thousands, and imitated, more or less shamelessly, during the past decade or so. Almost a compromise between exclusive luxury items and ubiquitous tourist trinkets. Who can say what Cristóbal Balenciaga might have thought of such a popular, if not downright democratic, success? Balenciaga became famous for his elitist and aristocratic vision of fashion, and his almost saintly veneration after more than fifty years as a couturier, as he retired from the fashion world in 1968, at a time when prêt-à-porter, the new way of mass consumption, was beginning to prevail as the savior of the fashion "industry." Most likely, he would have been unhappy, because nothing could be further from the mark he left on the history of fashion, than a most coveted mass-produced bag.

Cristóbal Balenciaga was born in Getaria, in the Basque country of Spain, in 1895. His father was a fisherman, and his mother worked as a seamstress for a noble family. A religious vocation as a young boy was replaced by one in fashion. It was the noblewoman, the Marquesa de Casa Torres, whom his mother served, who noticed him and who, taking him under her protective wing, enabled him to study dressmaking, in Madrid.

After that, his career took off and was continuously on the rise. In 1919, he opened his first boutique, in San Sebastián—the ladies of the country's aristocracy vied to wear his unique creations—where he established a reputation for exquisite precision and supreme artisanship. The civil war forced him to move to Paris, fashion capital of the world, where, in July of 1937, he founded his house of fashion at No.10, Avenue George V, which, for the next thirty years, became synonymous with the most exclusive and sophisticated creations, haute couture that was intended to be the union of quality and art. The greatest of Balenciaga's many contributions to haute couture might have been his radical approach to dressmaking, more than the realization of his own true style—his wish to take the art to its extremes.

30 The great couturier at work as he molds one of his patterns, with surgical precision, directly onto the body of a model.

31 One of Balenciaga's most famous items, a dress made of hundreds of tiny, artfully frayed, strips silk chiffon presented with a roomy cocoon overcoat.

Cristóbal BALENCIAGA

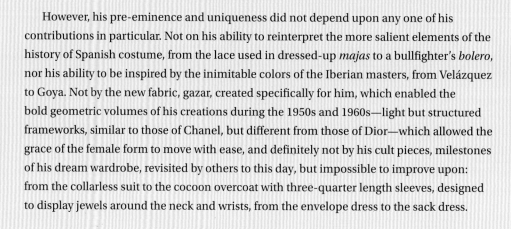

However, his pre-eminence and uniqueness did not depend upon any one of his contributions in particular. Not on his ability to reinterpret the more salient elements of the history of Spanish costume, from the lace used in dressed-up *majas* to a bullfighter's *bolero*, nor his ability to be inspired by the inimitable colors of the Iberian masters, from Velázquez to Goya. Not by the new fabric, gazar, created specifically for him, which enabled the bold geometric volumes of his creations during the 1950s and 1960s—light but structured frameworks, similar to those of Chanel, but different from those of Dior—which allowed the grace of the female form to move with ease, and definitely not by his cult pieces, milestones of his dream wardrobe, revisited by others to this day, but impossible to improve upon: from the collarless suit to the cocoon overcoat with three-quarter length sleeves, designed to display jewels around the neck and wrists, from the envelope dress to the sack dress.

Balenciaga was certainly all of these, but he was also something more, and something different. He represented the single-mindedness of following an absolute fashion ideal, in which the clothes spoke exclusively, and above everything else. Perfect and impeccable, made to measure, cut and sewn for the figure of the woman who will become their owner, rather than that vulgarity of mass-produced womenswear, tossed in a display window like any old merchandise. In addition, the couturier must be a step behind these, shun visibility, avoid self-exhibition, recoil from worldliness, and be dedicated, body and soul, to the obsessive and perhaps even pathological toils of a labor whose yardstick lies solely in perfection. The results are garments that require three or even four fittings, that are exorbitantly expensive and soberly elegant, that are concentrated and internalized, and never conspicuous.

Certainly, he was intent on contributing to the formation of his own myth, only releasing himself to his public in tiny doses; it is enough to recall that, throughout his life, he granted only one real interview. Nevertheless, even colleagues and journalists, whom he never cajoled, elevated him, in their public statements, to be in a radical "world apart," a place where he naturally belonged. Speaking of him, Coco Chanel said, "Balenciaga is a couturier in the truest sense of the word. Only he is capable of cutting material, assembling a creation, and sewing it by hand. The others are simply fashion designers." Christian Dior summarized it tersely, defining him as "the couturier of couturiers, the master of all of us." Diana Vreeland captured this sentiment with the image of grandeur: "when a woman dressed in Balenciaga enters a room, all the rest disappear."

32 Two white bows stand out from this all-black dress. The outfit dates from 1938, but its modernity is apparent, even today.

33 This immortal ensemble dates from 1951, that is, to the beginning of the golden age of the couturier's career—the softly draped dress has been paired—with an eggplant-colored overcoat.

34 At No. 10 Avenue George V, Balenciaga created unique, bespoke dresses, cut and sewn on the client.

35 Aristocratic and super-feminine, sensual but haughty: that is Cristóbal Balenciaga's idealized woman, like the model, here wearing one of his 1953 creations. A diamond choker by Van Cleef & Arpels underscores the outfit's opulence.

36 Three-quarter length sleeves for the lacquer-red suit, seemingly simple and severe, with matching pillbox hat and lipstick, while the gloves, immaculate white, accentuate the contrast. An abstract, almost supernatural, elegance that requires no superfluous frills to manifest itself.

"When a woman dressed in Balenciaga enters a room, all the rest disappear."
–Diana Vreeland

He was careful in his own defense: "no dressmaker can make a woman elegant," he said, "if she isn't so by nature." Simply, he was the favorite couturier of Grace Kelly, Lauren Bacall, Lee Radziwill and Helena Rubenstein.

His house survived his retirement, and his death, in 1972. There was a price to pay, however. In 1987, the label returned to the runway, under the creative direction first of Michel Goma, then, from 1992, of Josephus Thimister. In 1997, came the turn of the highly celebrated Nicolas Ghesquière, and, in 2012, of Alexander Wang. Now, the rules are different. Sell, sell, sell, is the order of the day. Even if only a bag.

37 Luxury ivory-hued fur coat, tone-on-tone with the dress, but contrasting with a graceful hat. The image, from 1953, once again highlights the extreme sophistication of the great Spanish couturier's approach to fashion.

Christian

Dior

THE EXPLOSION OCCURRED ON A SPECIFIC DAY AND AT A SPECIFIC MOMENT.
IT WAS ON FEBRUARY 12, 1947, AT 10:30 A.M. THAT THE "DIOR BOMB" EXPLODED—*NUMÉRO UN*,
THE FIRST OUTFIT, OF THE VERY FIRST COLLECTION SIGNED BY CHRISTIAN DIOR,
WAS ANNOUNCED.

In the private apartment of the House, No. 30, Avenue Montaigne in Paris, surrounded by white walls and Louis XVI style furnishings, an astonished audience witnessed a succession of 90 unprecedented, elongated, silhouettes, lines, and volumes, full rustling skirts, tapered waists, and seductive bodices. At the conclusion of the fashion parade, Carmel Snow, editor-in-chief of *Harper's Bazaar*, exclaimed: "My dear Christian, your outfits have such a new look!" A Reuters correspondent jotted the phrase down on a scrap of paper, which he then threw, from the window, to a waiting courier. News of the "New Look" arrived in the United States that same day, sooner even than it did the rest of France, where a newspaper strike had been dragging on for a month.

Actually, the 'novelty' to which Snow was referring was an unexpected return to the past. Two years after the war's end, Dior turned his back on rationing and gloom in order to relaunch Parisian high fashion with great pomp, and amid polemic as much as admiration, criticism, and elation, in order to restore fantasy and fairy tale to women. Dozens of meters of precious fabrics—15 for a skirt, a good 25 for an evening gown—enveloped a woman in luxury and femininity. The corset and the bodice, absent from the female wardrobe since Poiret and Coco Chanel's explosion on the fashion scene, made their reappearance.

The revolutionary "Corolle" line foresaw immense skirts, as fluffy as flowers in bloom, paired with waist-pinching little jacket-corsages, three-quarter length sleeves, and soft, rounded shoulders. The look was completed by accessories: flat, disk-like hats, long gloves, and sophisticated, high-heeled shoes which were utterly different from the square-toe, wedged ones worn by women in the audience at the fashion event. Everyone, from Marlene Dietrich—seated in the audience of this first show, and, henceforth, a muse and client of the House—to the regular aficionados, had a single desire: to adopt the New Look that Dior had defined as the "return to an ideal of civilized joy."

Christian Dior was 42 when he presented his first revolutionary collection, but his course had been set since his youth.

40 An evening outfit composed of a black satin skirt and a tight-waisted jacket with three-quarter length sleeves. One of the patterns in the famous Corolle line—tight waist, full skirt—hailed by the press as the "New Look."

41 Between walls of white linen, mirrors, and crystal chandeliers, journalists watch the final adjustment of a dress in the hotel at number 30 Avenue Montaigne, where Christian Dior established his base.

BORN IN 1905, IN GRANVILLE, ON THE COAST OF NORMANDY,
DIOR SPENT HIS CHILDHOOD AT "LES RHUMBS," THE FAMILY'S LARGE VILLA,
WHERE HE WAS FREE TO GIVE VENT TO HIS CREATIVE WHIMS BY DESIGNING
AND INVENTING COSTUMES AND FANCY DRESS. THE IDEAS HE ABSORBED
IN THIS PERIOD LATER ENTERED HIS AESTHETIC.

Ideas born in the villa's garden included the "flower-woman," the Corolle and Tulip Lines. While lilies-of-the-valley became the mascot and symbol of the House—stitched into the hems of its haute couture garments, worn by the designer in his buttonhole, or enclosed in a bottle of Diorissimo (the House's first perfume, created in 1948), red poppies, orange nasturtiums, yellow daffodils, pink peonies... inspired the color palette of his later creations. Everything bore a sign, everything had a meaning. Christian Dior believed in fate and in premonition. Reading his fabulous future as a couturier in his palm, a fortuneteller told the fourteen year-old: "You will find yourself without money, but women will help you, and it is thanks to them that you will make a fortune."

In Paris, to embark on a diplomatic career in accordance with his parents' wishes, the twenty-year-old Dior hung out with the great artists of the time. After abandoning his studies in political science, he became director of an art gallery in association with Jean Bonjean. At 34 Rue de la Boétie he dealt in works by the most celebrated—or soon to be the most celebrated—artists of the time: Paul Klee, Salvador Dalí, Joan Miro, Giorgio De Chirico, and Pablo Picasso. Forced to close the gallery after the bankruptcy of his father's business and his mother's death, Dior entered a long period of financial hardship during which he eked out a living by selling sketches to fashion houses and contributing his drawings to *Le Figaro Illustré*. In 1938, he began working for the House of Piguet. That fateful encounter in April 1946, allowed destiny to be fulfilled. The forty-one-year-old Christian Dior was working in the atelier of Lucien Lelong. It was the textile industry tycoon Marcel Boussace, who, noticing him, offered to finance his studio. Thus, the House of Dior was born.

From the announcement of his very first design-collection, season after season, Christian Dior dictated the rules of dress, offering his clientele ever more innovative looks. The Corolle and Huit lines, were followed by the H (with an even narrower waist), the A, the Y, the Tulip, and finally the *Fuseau* line—transitioning from the rounded silhouettes of the 1950s to the straight lines of the 1960s. Enhancing the feminine quality of his creations were feathers, fine lacework and tricot, black, white and pink polka dots, and animal patterns—his passion—in the form of leopard skin inserts on coat cuffs and pillbox hats, or printed upon evening and day wear.

Ten years—from 1947-1957—were enough for the brilliant designer to transform his name into a dream label, a fashion empire, ranging from haute couture to accessories, from jewelry to perfumes, with boutiques all over the world. Christian Dior died in a hotel, in Montecatini, in the summer of 1957. Taking over his artistic legacy, was his very young assistant, the twenty-one-year-old Yves Saint Laurent, a child prodigy of French high fashion, who had created the Trapeze collection for Dior, and later the very concept of prêt-à-porter fashion. But that is another story.

43 A model dressed in a fabulous strapless, black velvet evening gown in November 1949. White gloves, precious jewels, and a fan accentuate the look.

44 Dior, in February 1957, in his legendary white lab coat, adding finishing touches to one of his evening gowns. He died that summer.

45 A model from the 1956 H line. This supremely elegant and ultra-refined silhouette was adopted by Grace Kelly, the couturier's client and muse.

46 From his 1947 debut, the couturier was both criticized and venerated for his unrestrained use of fabric. Indeed, dozens of meters of organza, silk, tulle, and costly textiles might be needed to create just one Dior.

47 Cocktail outfits and fabulous evening gowns: this image captures Dior's entire repertoire. From the Corolle line to the H line and all the way to the sack coat line.

Emilio
PUCCI

EMILIO PUCCI, MARQUIS OF BARSENTO—A MAN OF CREATIVE AND INNOVATIVE TALENT, A PIONEER IN 1950S ITALIAN FASHION, AND OF THE IDEA OF PRÊT-À-PORTER, A SUBLIME CREATOR OF UNMISTAKABLE PRINTS INSPIRED BY POP ART, AND AN ORIGINAL, AND REVOLUTIONARY, RANGE OF COLORS—ENTERED FASHION BY ACCIDENT.

The first thirty years of his life, as a Florentine nobleman, did not presage his future as a designer. Certainly, as a college student in the United States, and a ski champion, the young Emilio did not imagine that he would enter history, not as a Marquis but as the "Prince of Prints"—a title far more important because it was acquired through talent. Even less, could anyone have foreseen that Emilio Pucci, a courageous pilot during the Second World War, would, one day, become known all over the world for the colors and kaleidoscopic fantasies of his clothing designs?

Born in Naples, in 1914, Emilio Pucci belonged to a noble family of ancient lineage. After studying social sciences in Athens, Georgia, and Portland, Oregon, on an athletic scholarship that allowed him to train as a skier, he enlisted in the Regia Aeronautica Italiana (the Italian Airforce, renamed Aeronautica Militare Italiana, after Italy became a Republic), in 1938. Granted a diploma in political science in Florence, he had a distinguished military career during the Second World War.

How did clothing come to be part of the Florentine aristocrat's life? *A la mode*, we would say. Pucci came upon it by chance. Everything began with a ski-suit he designed for an aristocratic friend, in 1947.

Emilio, a war veteran, found himself in Zermatt, where he was training as a member of the Olympic ski team. As a joke, he put together an innovative, aerodynamic sports suit. It was Toni Frissell, renowned photographer of *Harper's Bazaar,* who noticed the outfit and immortalized it in the American magazine's glossy pages. It was such a hit in the United States that Pucci was inspired to create a line of women's clothing. His creations were marketed overseas under the label "Emilio" in order to protect the family name. "I was the first member of my family to work in a 1000 years," he told *Life* magazine, in 1964.

Another fashionable vacation resort served as the backdrop for the emergence of his beach collection. Pucci opened his first boutique in Capri, making his debut with a line of clothing items in printed silk. Within a short time, the entire coast of the Mediterranean was dotted with his explosive prints—as colorful and lively as the sea, and the luxurious vegetation of the region.

50 Emilio Pucci, Marquis of Barsento at work in his atelier located in the family residence: Palazzo Pucci on via de' Pucci in Florence.

51 The innovative uniform created by Emilio Pucci for the cabin staff of American airline, Braniff International. Between 1965 and 1977 he revolutionized the uniform, bringing fashion to scheduled flights.

To cope with ever more pressing demand, he founded an artisanal workshop in his family home, Palazzo Pucci on Via de' Pucci in Florence. There, inspired by the art and history of Italy, he created progressively more incredible prints. Among the most famous are the *Siciliana* collection (1956), the *Palio di Siena* (1957)—with heraldic devices depicting the traditional horse race—and another dedicated to Botticelli. Pucci codified color after color until he had a palette of over 80 hues, as well as combinations of them that included up to sixteen in a single pattern.

In the early 1960s, there was not a socialite worthy of the name who did not own a Pucci. From men's shirts to slacks, from scarves to fluttering evening gowns, there was nothing that he did not create for his fans, among whom could be counted Jacqueline Kennedy and Marilyn Monroe. But what won him true fame was the silk jersey dress—light as a feather, taking up virtually no space, and, most importantly, wrinkle-free—which became the uniform of the chic globetrotters of the international jet set. Pucci's interest in experimenting with fabrics also gave birth to 'Emilioform,' a special, comfortable, light, stretch fabric made of helanca (a textured yarn) and shantung silk, of which *Viva* pants with gaiters—a further development of the leggings invented by Pucci himself—were made.

Pucci's travels to South America, Asia, Indonesia, and Australia with his wife Cristina exposed the designer to even more amazing colors, and new geometric patterns. As a result, an "exotic" theme surfaced in his first high fashion collection in 1962, which stood out for its precious materials, and Swarovski crystal adornments, applied by hand to his *Palazzo* pajamas. 1968 saw a deal signed with Ermenegildo Zegna and a decision to launch a men's line. A man of eclectic creative talent, Pucci agreed, in the late 1960s, to design the stewardess uniforms for Braniff International Airways, while in 1971, he was commissioned by NASA to design the logo of the Apollo 15 space mission.

With the rise of disco-casual fashion in the 1970s, and men's cut apparel favored by the 1980s "Power Woman," Puccimania came to a standstill. Laudomia Pucci assumed the company's reins after the death of her father. Since 2000, the year in which 67% of the company was acquired by the luxury colossus LVMH (Louis Vuitton Moët Hennessy), various talented figures have alternated in the role of artistic advisor, among them Christian Lacroix and Matthew Williamson. Yet it was only with the arrival of Peter Dundas, in 2008, that Pucci reverted to its splendid beginnings. This young brilliant designer, of Norwegian origin, immediately showed himself capable of revitalizing the chic Bohemian spirit created by the firm's founder, and of reviving it in accordance with the rules of contemporary fashion.

52 A taste for exoticism, which arose from the designer's travels with his wife, is a recurring theme in Pucci's collections. In this case, harem pants and Indian slippers complement a blouse bearing one of the House's unmistakable prints.

53 It was the colors and patterns of pop-art-inspired clothing that earned Pucci the title "Prince of Prints." This sample, in silk, from 1966 is just one example.

Pierre
CARDIN

"I ASKED MYSELF: WHY CAN ONLY THE RICH HAVE ACCESS TO EXCLUSIVE FASHION?
WHY CAN'T THE MAN OR WOMAN IN THE STREET HAVE IT AS WELL?
I HAD THE POWER TO CHANGE THAT RULE, AND I DID."

PIERRE CARDIN DESERVES A SPECIAL PLACE IN THE HISTORY OF FASHION. AT A TIME WHEN NO ONE COULD HAVE IMAGINED SUCH A THING, HE TOOK A RISK THAT, UNTIL THEN, WOULD HAVE BEEN UNTHINKABLE, AND, AFTER WHICH, THE ENTIRE FASHION WORLD HAD TO COPE WITH THE DEMANDS OF A NEW WAY OF THINKING AS A RESULT OF MOMENTOUS CHANGE.

The year was 1959, and he had created a prêt-à-porter collection specifically for the Parisian department-store chain, Le Printemps, whose clientele was unfamiliar with the exclusivity of haute couture. His approach was clearly not that of stealing trends off the street, as do many of today's designers, only to hand them back in a deluxe version on their runways, but rather, the exact opposite, namely, that of bringing the designer's creativity to as large a public as possible, with precisely what which fills department stores and city streets. "I did this for an economic reason," he explained without beating around the bush. "I was always losing loads of money with Haute Couture. And for an ideological reason: being on the left, I wanted a fashion that was accessible to everyone, not only the rich."

This also proved to be true. It is a fact that, thanks to this intuition, and all those that followed, Cardin grew wealthier and wealthier. He found himself at the head of an empire, which, over the decades, in addition to apparel, offered hotels, deluxe restaurants, spas, and prestigious buildings including the Palais Bulles in Cannes, the futuristic architecture of Antti Lovag, and the Ca' Bragadin hotel in Venice, where, he proudly boasts, Giacomo Casanova used to live. With the wealth that his empire brought him, Cardin indulged in the luxury of pursuing bold stylistic experiments, on the one hand, and perfecting his innovative business models, which proved extremely profitable for a while, on the other. Cardin "invented" a system of licenses, (900 or so in his case), that allowed him to "lease" his name to other companies. His name became linked to many disparate commodities, from home appliances to silverware, and from furniture to cigarette lighters, and with it, he was able to 'invade' untouched markets, such as Japan and China in the Far East, where Cardin was a real export pioneer.

Cardin paid a heavy price for his desire to unhinge the system, disrupt the game, and provoke a scandal by overthrowing the status quo; his 1959 "democratic" collection did not go down well with the Chambre Syndicale de la Mode, which actually expelled him for a brief period. Nevertheless, the temptation to look ahead, to think of the possibility of a different future (or a different idea of a future) was too radically rooted in his DNA. Today, as ever, Pierre Cardin is an affable and supremely elegant man who has proudly passed the threshold of 90, and who still allows himself the privilege of dreaming big. His most recent project (shelved due to polemics and also the huge monster of Italian bureaucracy) was to build a futuristic skyscraper, the Palais Lumière, near Venice—a multi-digit investment with which Cardin could have given something back to the place where his life had begun in 1922.

56 Mother and daughter models Biki and Betsy, present two patterns from Pierre Cardin's 1996-1967 Fall/Winter collection. The A-line coat is paired with a futuristic headdress: a fashion that looks to the future.

57 The designer adding finishing touches to one of his 1967 creations. Geometrical lines and basic color combinations. The designer's monogram stands out visibly from the dress, at the peak of his career.

He was born Pietro Cardini in Sant'Andrea di Barbarana, to a farming family from Treviso that had fallen on hard times after the First World War, and thus had moved to France to seek its fortune, when Pietro—who became Pierre—was only four years old.

Cardin worked for Jeanne Paquin and Elsa Schiaparelli, but his lucky break came in 1947, when Christian Dior hired him as his chief garment-cutter. Though Cardin instigated the birth of the revolutionary New Look, fashion was not his only interest. He also loved the theater, and has collaborated with Jean Cocteau and Christian Bérard. Throughout his life, he has dedicated himself to supporting talented young actors, offering them hospitality in his Espace Pierre Cardin in Paris, and organizing numerous theater festivals.

In 1950, he founded his house of fashion, with André Olivier. In 1953, he designed his first collection, which already contained the essence of the style that he was to pursue throughout his career and that objectified his curious approach to life. Cardin's fashion is futuristic, spatial, forward-looking, dominated by daring geometries, shocking colors, and basic, extreme and bizarre lines. Emanating from genie lamps, it sometimes, perhaps, borders on kitsch—as in the case of his celebrated *robes bulles*, a dress designed with a compass, and more of a work of art than a garment to be worn. With his fashion, Cardin traveled to the moon well before Neil Armstrong and even Barbarella. He discovered women's legs well before Mary Quant. He predicted globalization well before 'No' logos criticized it.

His mantra is "look ahead," and, even today, he does not seem to have any intention of stopping.

58 Cardin at work in his London store, in 1970. The geometric print fabric that he works with is typical of the era but still in vogue today thanks to its simplicity and his rigor.

59 Denise Cox models one of Pierre Cardin's signature creations, in 1970, at the Dickins & Jones department store in London. The ensemble, a wool dress and cape, is a marvelous example of the geometric style that made the designer world famous.

60 One year before the Moon Landing, Cardin introduced futuristic "space" items, such as these three garments from 1968, which came with boots and long gloves.

61 Cardin's basic, and completely unaffected, style of the mid-1960s. The trapeze dress, available in two metallic shades, is paired with the simplicity of flat shoes.

62 Decades pass, but Pierre Cardin's style remains unchanged. In 2012, once again, we find bold geometries and vibrant colors on the runway, as in this elaboration of the classic *Little Black Dress sui generis*.

63 In 2011, Pierre Cardin's fashion appeared on a runway at the Kremlin. The optical effect and wonder that this colorful sculpted dress is able to generate matter much more than its wearability.

Hubert de
GIVENCHY

"PERSONALLY I DEPEND ON GIVENCHY THE WAY AMERICAN WOMEN DEPEND
ON THEIR PSYCHIATRISTS." —AUDREY HEPBURN

THE NAME ITSELF EVOKES REFINEMENT, GRACE, AND SIMPLICITY,
THE QUALITIES OF THE CLOTHING THAT GIVENCHY CREATED AND THOSE PHYSICAL
AND SPIRITUAL QUALITIES OF THE DESIGNER HIMSELF.

A man of innate and elegant taste, Count Hubert James Marcel Taffin de Givenchy was, in 1952, the year of his collection's debut, among the youngest couturiers in Paris. Tall, handsome, elegant, and barely 17 years of age, he had arrived in Paris after the War to study design at the École des Beaux Arts. Despite his family's opposition to his desire to become a couturier, Givenchy worked as an apprentice to Jacques Fath, the youngest and most imaginative dressmaker of the time, and then in the ateliers of Robert Piguet and Lucien Lelong. But it was Elsa Schiaparelli's studio that truly shaped him; four years at a unique atelier with an iconic designer who influenced his style, which always combined elegance and perfectionism with a twist of originality.

The debut of Maison Givenchy, in 1952, happened when the designer was 25 years old. Triumph came immediately. Every magazine spoke of his Bettina blouse, a simple white cotton shirt that took its name from the most celebrated runway model of the time, Bettina Graziani.

The encounter that sealed the House's destiny occurred the following year. It was in 1953 that Audrey Hepburn requested a visit to the designer's atelier. Givenchy was at work on his new collection, but believing that he was dealing with the other, more famous, Hepburn, Katherine, he agreed. Both were struck by lightning. Audrey asked the young couturier to design her wardrobe for *Sabrina* (1954), and he showed her some samples that seemed cut explicitly for her. From that moment on, the actress wore nothing but Givenchy, on or off the set; she became the icon of an impeccable and chic style, vital and refined, an ambassador of Givenchy elegance, betting more on subtraction and reserve than on ostentation. Together, the couturier and the actress created the 'Audrey Hepburn style.' Their partnership engendered those unforgettable movie moments: the princess silhouette of Sabrina's black and white full-skirted dress which was to be merely the prelude to a series of creations that culminated in the most iconic creation in cinematic history, the black turban immortalized in *Breakfast at Tiffany's* (1961).

66 Audrey Hepburn, in Billy Wilder's *Sabrina* (1954). The white organza dress, embroidered with the silhouette of the princess, was purchased in the atelier of a still very young Hubert de Givenchy.

67 Givenchy in his atelier observing three prêt-à-porter items in (left to right) black alpaca, pink canvas, and grey flannel.

Under the protective wing of Cristóbal Balenciaga, his mentor and friend, and his neighbor on Avenue George V, Givenchy focused ever more on purity of line and 'architectural' cuts. "From him I learned that one never needed to cheat either in life or in work," he recalled when interviewed by Maria Pezzi for *Donna* magazine—"that a button with five holes was useless when one with four was enough, or one flower more."

The 1950s and 1960s were Givenchy's golden age. The designer introduced the sack dress (1953), the coat with wraparound collar (1958), the balloon skirt, and the corset dress (1969). In 1968, Balenciaga retired, and Givenchy inherited his prestigious clientele, from Lauren Bacall to the Duchess of Windsor, from Jean Sebert to Princess Grace of Monaco and Jacqueline Kennedy.

In 1988, Givenchy was acquired by French multinational LVMH (Louis Vuitton Moët Hennessy), but the designer did not hang up his white coat (his habitual work uniform) until 1995, after his final show. Since then various talented individuals have taken turns as Givenchy creative director: John Galliano, Alexander McQueen, both more provocative and shocking, then Julien Macdonald, Italian Riccardo Tisci, and, finally, Sebastian Suhl, formerly of Prada. None of them, however, has seemed to live up to the challenge of assuming the legacy of the founder, that ineffable elegance based on the principle that "the classic is never boring."

68 The partnership between Hepburn and Givenchy gave birth to some of the most iconic outfits in cinema history. Most iconic of all being Holly Golightly's little black dress in *Breakfast at Tiffany's* (1961).

69 The friendship and esteem shared by the actress and couturier lasted a lifetime. In the opening scene of *How to Steal a Million* (1966), the cap, tied beneath Hepburn's chin, and the white sunglasses, epitomized her look.

70 A 1953 suit consisting of a full skirt with an Orient-inspired print, a lace petticoat, and a little satin jacket.

71 Three interchangeable tops and skirts that the designer introduced together, in order to create a variety of outfits.

72 Model Bettina Graziani, the muse who inspired the cult Bettina shirt, wearing an embroidered dress with a white jacket edged with a black fringe.

73 Wool overcoat with full, puffed sleeves, accentuated with accessories: a cloche hat and a tote bag.

74 A black tulle dress with tone-on-tone dots from the prêt-à-porter 1991 Spring/Summer collection.

75 A sample from the 1991 Spring/Summer collection. The dress, in a colorful butterfly print, has a bow at the back

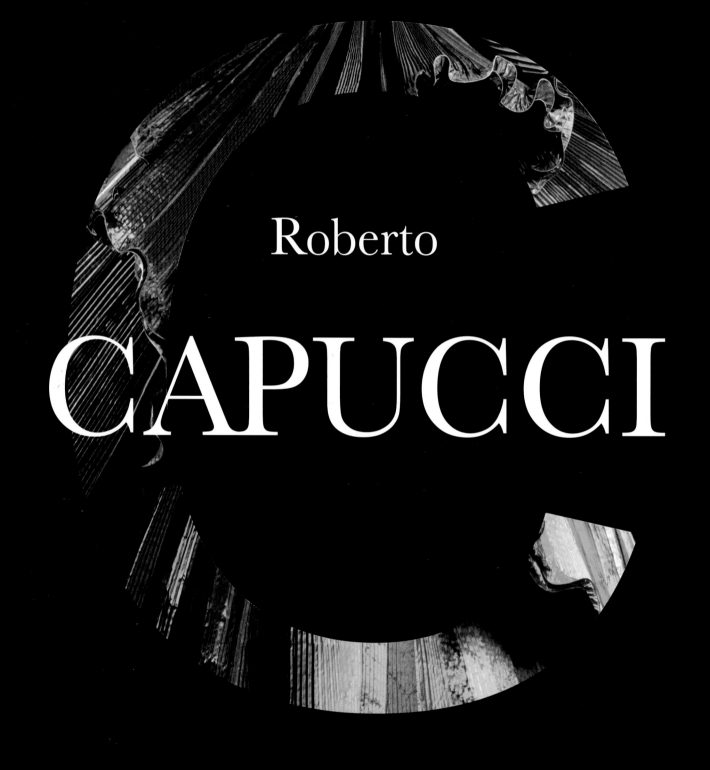

Roberto
CAPUCCI

"IF I COULD, I WOULD ELIMINATE THE TERM 'FASHION' FROM THE DICTIONARY."
"TO BE IN FASHION IS ALREADY TO BE OUT OF FASHION."

78 A very young Roberto Capucci, surrounded by his sketches, in 1958.

79 Actress Esther Williams tries on the famous "Nine Skirts" dress in Capucci's atelier.

"FASHION IS NOT AN ORNAMENT, IT'S ARCHITECTURE.
IT'S NOT ENOUGH FOR A DRESS TO BE BEAUTIFUL, IT MUST BE CONSTRUCTED LIKE A BUILDING,
THIS IS THE MATERIALIZATION OF AN IDEA."

The art training he received at the Academy of Fine Arts in Rome, where he was the pupil of Carlo Mazzacurati, Stella de Libero, and Alessandro Avenali, influenced the entire career of Roberto Capucci. His work, like art, is free, his creativity is independent of the seasonal changes in fashion.

Born in the Rome in 1930, Capucci was the child prodigy of Italian fashion and only twenty when he opened his first atelier. In 1951, he participated, "unofficially," in the first round of collective exhibitions of Italian fashion that were organized, in Florence, by Giovanni Battista Giorgini. "My youth," recalls Capucci, "was a barrier to my official participation in the show. Despite this and thanks to his esteem for me, Giorgini asked me to dress his wife and two daughters for the occasion. It was a bomb. Journalists and buyers were enthralled by their elegance, and thus what was supposed to have been done on the sly, concluded with a buzz, and this "non-participation" was transformed, without any intention, into my first great success, which was followed by enthusiastic reviews and huge orders for clothing."

From the outset, the young designer demonstrated an interest in form and structure. Spirals, circles, ribbing, and pleats drew inspiration from surrealist painting and from cubist work, but above all from nature, which he found endlessly fascinating. According to the couturier, the perfection and harmony of the universe could be traced in tiny things: a leaf glistening with raindrops, a bird in flight, a flower, a beehive, even the concentric ripples created by a stone cast in water which actually inspired his celebrated "Nine Skirts" (1956), a red silk taffeta dress achieving worldwide fame after being worn by Hollywood star Esther Williams.

Acclaimed by the international press, he even received praise from Christian Dior: "In Italy, you have a prodigious boy called Roberto Capucci; if he happens to be in Paris, he must come and find me." The encounter never took place because the great French couturier died in 1957, whereas Capucci did not arrive in the so-called "*Ville Lumière*" ("*City of Light*") until 1962.

Achieving more popularity after his invention of the boxy silhouette line, which earned him the fashion Oscar from the Boston department store, Filene's, Capucci opened a second atelier in the vicinity of the Eiffel Tower. His experiments with high-tech plastic fibers, Plexiglas and metal, and the further refinement of his dressmaking technique date to his years in Paris. Returning to Italy in 1968, he initiated a new fashion trend. Influenced by the movement known as '*arte povera*,' which arose in Italy in the mid-1970s, he added to his range of unusual materials: straw, raffia, bamboo, and rope, strung together with luxurious haute couture fabrics such as fine silk and georgette.

His creations left the diktats of the then fashion world farther and farther behind. His need for creative freedom, which made him more of an artist than a designer, induced him to disengage himself, definitively, from the fashion industry in the early 1980s. He decided to stop putting on shows, according to the rigid calendar set by the Chamber of Italian Fashion, and to devote himself entirely to study.

His works, ever more dreamlike and regal, began traveling the world, from Rome to New York, from Tokyo to Beijing; always presented in unusual locations, they revealed their beauty in museum galleries, palaces, academies, and theatres. The 1995 Venice Bienniale devoted an entire hall to the creations of this Roman couturier.

His dresses are unique, works of art that may require as many as four months of labor and 180 meters of fabric.

Exorbitantly expensive textiles, such as sarcenet, taffeta, fabrics hand-woven on sixteenth-century looms, raw silk, georgette and mikado, are transformed by his hands into dynamic forms and volumes. The designer-sculptor has also turned his research to color. Up to 172 shades of the same color might appear, with incredible chromatic effect, in the tiny pleats of one of his skirts or bodices—as in the plissé dress, in 37 shades of blue, inspired by the ocean, and exhibited in the Italian pavilion at the Lisbon Expo in 1998.

In his time, he has created fairy-tale couture for princesses, intellectuals, artists, and such movie stars as Marilyn Monroe, Gloria Swanson, and Silvana Mangano. The last of these, the most elegant of all according to the Roman couturier, wore Capucci in Pier Paolo Pasolini's *Teorema* (1968), while Rita Levi di Montalcini received her Noble Prize for Medicine dressed in a black silk Capucci with a short train.

Wearable sculpture that does not need the support of a body to bring it to life. "Discreet, haughty, perhaps slightly annoyed by the body's chatter," notes Giovanni Mariotti in an essay on the designer, "they live at ease in the reserve of Beauty and Culture, like lions on the savannah."

81 The classic red shift is accentuated by the addition of a flared skirt composed of nine layers of silk taffeta. Purchased by Williams in 1957, the "Nine Skirts" dress was reproduced that same year in a comic strip dedicated to Marilyn Monroe.

82 The designer's love of nature culminated with the "Ocean" dress of 1998, composed of 1200 fragments of taffeta pleated in 37 shades of blue.

83 Capucci's dresses are works of art, created without regard to cost or wearability. Inspiration often comes from his study of minerals, flowers, or butterflies, as in the case of the "Butterfly" dress.

84 The designer has his textiles dyed in Lyon, sometimes using a seemingly infinite number of hues in a single garment.

85 Three items in multicolored, pleated, silk taffeta created with an origami effect.

VALENTINO Garavani

FOR ANY OTHER DESIGNER THE EPITHET "EMPEROR" WOULD HAVE CERTAINLY BEEN AN EXAGGERATION, AND, POSSIBLY, EVEN RIDICULOUS. BUT NOT FOR VALENTINO CLEMENTE LUDOVICO GARAVANI, BORN IN VOGHERA, LOMBARDY, IN 1932, AND KNOWN TO THE WORLD, LIKE ALL THE GREAT EMPERORS, BY ONLY HIS FIRST NAME.

When one is so grand and unmistakable, the last name is simply "superfluous." The fame of the couturier is, essentially, universal, and his colleagues do not miss an opportunity to demonstrate their respect, esteem, admiration, and deference, in a way, of the kind one feels before emperors.

Valentino, The Last Emperor (2008), the 'last' also in a profound sense, signifying the end—perhaps a definitive one—of the grand era of couture, was the title of an enjoyable documentary produced by journalist Matt Tyrnauer, the cherry on the cake of that endless series of events, festivities, and commemorations with which, in celebration of his 45 years in fashion, the master bade farewell to the scene. His label continues to thrive, designed, for a brief interval, by Alessandra Facchinetto and, today, by a pair of his faithful collaborators, Maria Grazia Chiuri and Pier Paolo Piccioli.

He, the Emperor, officially saluted everyone, in tears, on September 4, 2007, and then retired, so to speak, to the privacy of his simultaneously ostentatious and reserved life, between worldly commitments and public appearances. He goes skiing in Gstaad, enjoys the magnificence of his castle in Wideville, and hugs his inseparable pugs in Crespières. He left the party—as he himself said—when it was still full of people.

What remains is his ageless style. The consequences of his unceasing quest for beauty. His unmistakable class. The grace of his incredible creations—marvelous examples of absolute harmony—that go beyond time, fashion, or trends. If there is a feature that makes Valentino's work unique and special, perhaps it is the one that ought to be, but often is not, the underlying basis of any couturier's work: the will, above all other things, to exalt the pure and simple beauty of women.

In his almost 50 years in fashion, Valentino never allowed himself to be tempted by the lure of provocation, never ceded to the ephemeral allure of trends, never took the simplest and quickest route, that of distinction at all costs, or of novelty as an end in itself.

89 A young Valentino Garavani, with seamstresses, in his Rome atelier in 1958.

88 Valentino Garavani and Giancarlo Giammetti, the designer's right-hand man and companion of 12 years, in 1982 in front of a sketch-covered wall in their atelier.

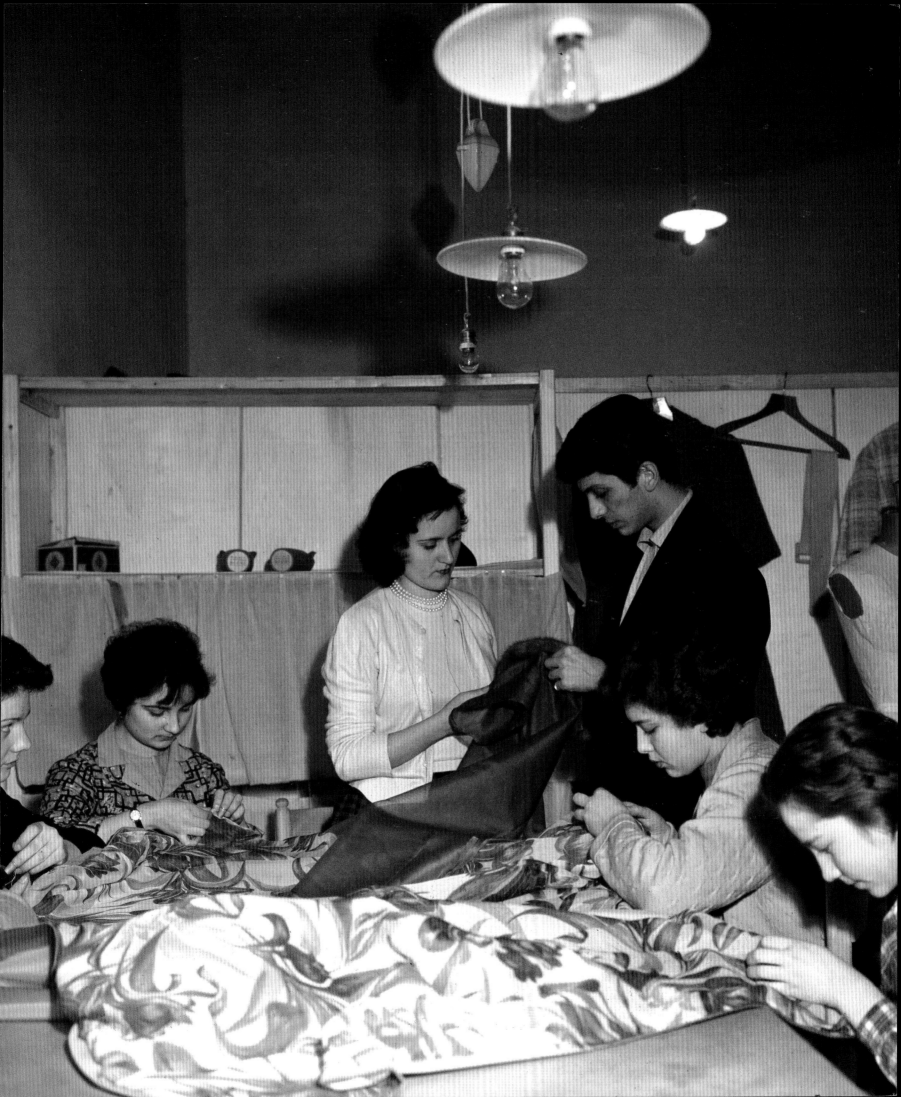

91 A long white dress created in 1990, during the Gulf War, with the word "peace" embroidered in 14 languages.

A mission—his mission—had been clear to him since his early youth. He was only a boy when he made a dress for his aunt. Yet he realized that it was fashion that would become his path in life only when he decided to attend a school for fashion sketching, in Milan, and above all, at age 17, when he departed for the fashion world capital, Paris. There, he underwent training at the atelier of Jean Dessès and Guy Laroche, where he learned to cut and sew with absolute mastery. As soon as he felt ready to embark on a solo career, he returned to Italy, to Rome, where he founded his house on Via Condotti, thanks to the help of his father and a group of associates. That was in 1960. Success did not come immediately. Yet Valentino, despite the good manners that also made him a master of *bon ton*, had a great deal of drive and tenacity and was by no means a quitter.

His lucky encounter with Giancarlo Giammetti, a student of architecture with an excellent sixth sense for business, marketing, and communication, as well as the designer's right-hand man and lifelong companion, allowed him to form a bond, which, from then on, reaped nothing but success after success. The first one, the label's breakthrough, was in 1962, and occurred in Florence, at the Palazzo Pitti, where Valentino participated in the final event on the last day of carnival, an exhibition promoting Italian fashion, conceived by Marquise Giovanni Battista Giorgini. An hour into the show, his collection was sold out. He was especially popular in the United States, where high society seemed particularly ready to receive the couturier's message, and where he was always mobbed and greeted in triumph.

90 In this 1968 image, the set for Valentino's creations is American artist Cy Twombly's Rome apartment. The models wear long silk evening gowns, and jackets with lace and pearl adornments on the cuffs.

From that moment on, his career spiraled endlessly upward. In 1968, he certainly did not commemorate the student revolts, but focused instead on his iconic white collection, which impressed itself on the collective imagination. Even a "certain" Jacqueline Lee Bouvier chose an immaculate white dress by the designer, whom she faithfully and assiduously admired, for her marriage to the Greek tycoon, Aristotle Onassis.

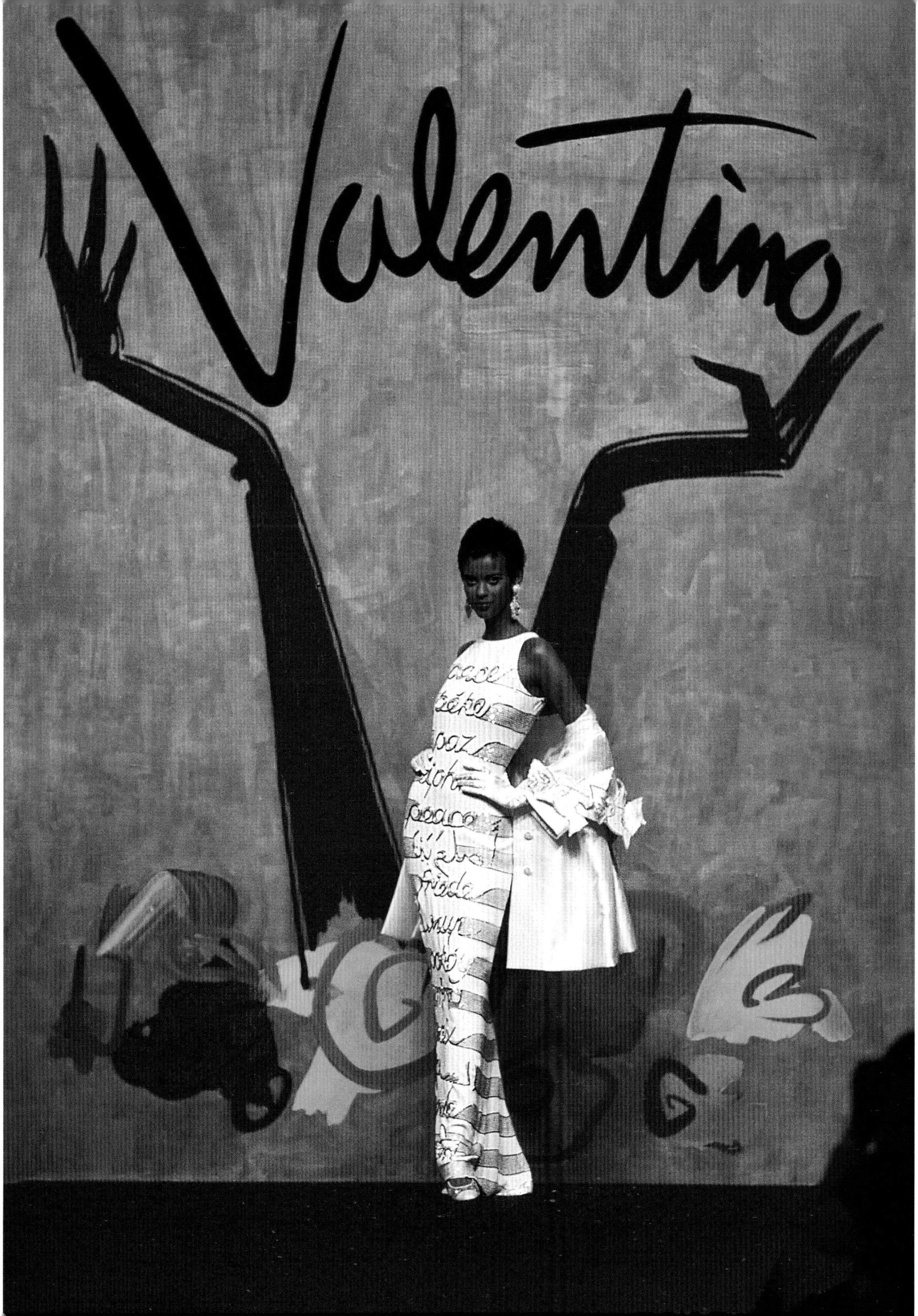
Valentino

YET, IT IS WITH ANOTHER HUE THAT THE COUTURIER'S LAVISH STYLE IS IDENTIFIED: THE LEGENDARY VALENTINO RED,

a particularly warm shade of the color, with a touch of orange, that inspired the designer at the first show he attended in Barcelona, when he was only 20, and which, like a good-luck charm, he never, afterward, omitted from the runway.

He dressed the most prestigious, aristocratic, refined and snobbish women of "good society" perfectly, as if in gift-wrap, in ribbons, frills, flowers, and magnificent bows. Never over the top. On the contrary, forever respecting the rules of dressing well, with devotion, deference, and conviction. Fearing neither opulence nor ostentation because he was perfectly capable of dominating both with good measure, his most distinctive stylistic feature.

92 Paris, January 23, 2008: 45 years after establishing his House, Valentino pays his moving farewell to the runway with an unforgettable array of "Valentino red" dresses.

93 The 2005-2006 Fall/Winter prêt-à-porter collection, presented in Paris, closes with a red silk evening gown bearing a train and a bow at the waist. A classic that carries the unmistakable signature of Valentino but, nonetheless, demonstrates a trend typical of that season: the taste for the Victorian Era.

94 Elite model Christy Turlington wearing a spectacular feather-bedecked floral headdress on the runway of the 1991-1992 Fall/Winter collection.

95 A dress from the 2007 Spring/Summer prêt-à-porter collection. The elegance of Italy and the absolute skill of this master of femininity are on view in the pleats of its bodice and the delicate flounces of its skirt.

96 Created with the precious labor of 40 seamstresses, at work in his Rome atelier, Valentino's dresses are masterpieces of exquisite design. Among the techniques that have contributed to the history of the House, is the "book-leaf" effect—organza disks sewn together to resemble the pages of a book.

97 The 2007-2008 Fall/Winter collection, presented in the Incisa and Baglivi halls of the 12th-century Borgo Santo Spirito in Sassia church, during the celebrations held in honor of the House's 45th anniversary, in July 2007. A lesson in sartorial elegance, refinement, and glamor.

VALENTINO
The Last Emperor

98 A view of the *Ara Pacis* during the opening of Valentino's great retrospective exhibition in Rome, "45 Years of Style." In a dialogue between past and present, the "Valentino red" dresses are set against the tunics of the magistrates, priests and Vestal Virgins carved into the Ara's marble.

99 One of the creations signed by the designer in the *Ara Pacis* exhibition. On view were sixty or so dresses worn by such icons as Jackie Kennedy, Audrey Hepburn, Cate Blanchett and Julia Roberts.

Karl
LAGERFELD

"FASHION IS LIKE MUSIC: SO MANY NOTES WITH WHICH TO PLAY.
AND EACH ONE CAN COMPOSE ITS OWN LITTLE MELODY."

"FASHION IS THE HEALTHIEST REASON FOR LOSING WEIGHT." "THE DEBATE OVER FURS IS CHILDISH." "ONLY FAT PEOPLE DO NOT LIKE THE THIN MODELS THAT WALK THE RUNWAY."

"If I were a woman in Russia I would be a lesbian because the men are so ugly." "Adele—a bit too fat." "Pippa Middleton—should only show side B; I don't like her face." "François Hollande—a moron who hates the rich."

One could fill entire pages with famous quips by Karl Lagerfeld—at least 176 of them, according to French journalists Jean-Christophe Napias, Patrick Mauriès, and Charles Ameline who have collected them all in their book, *Le Monde Selon Karl*. Although he later retracted his insult of François Hollande, and gave Adele an entire set of Chanel handbags to say he was sorry, the designer is universally known for his political incorrectness. Venomous and irreverent, Karl Lagerfeld does not mince his words. Aphorisms and cutting barbs, but also a great deal of self-irony, have helped make the Chanel designer an icon, as venerated as a rock star.

Grey hair and a pony tail, fingerless gloves, dark glasses (which he calls his burka) complete his outfit, making him a universally recognizable figure, "a living label," "a signature who walks," as he, himself, professes. "I am a caricature of myself, and this makes me happy. It's like wearing a mask. For me, the Venice carnival lasts all year round." And he lends the mask, Karl, to brands and projects of all kinds that are not necessarily related to fashion.

Born in Hamburg in 1938 (or 1933, or perhaps 1935, his date of birth is shrouded in a veil of mystery) to a wealthy, upper bourgeois family, Karl Otto Lagerfeldt (that trailing 't' was part of his name, which he later discarded, claiming that his name, without it, was more "commercial") moved to Paris when he was only 17 years old.

There, after completing secondary school, he astounded everybody with his drawing ability and began collaborating with several fashion houses. He won the Woolmark Prize, a competition organized by the International Wool Secretariat.

The overcoat he designed for the occasion was manufactured by Pierre Balmain, who, struck by the dropout's talent, employed him as his assistant. Three years later he was appointed artistic director of Maison Patou. But his free and restless spirit had problems tolerating the restrictive and elitist atmosphere of high fashion clothes makers. These were the early years of prêt-à-porter, and Lagerfeld was working as a freelance designer in France, Italy, England, and Germany. In Paris, it was for Chloé, in Rome he refurbished furs for Fendi, a collaboration with the Italian firm that began in 1965, and has continued to this day. In the meantime, he came up with his own style, which, since 1984, has been expressed by the label that bears his name. A volcanic talent. "Paid mercenary with a fixed honorarium." In an interview for *La Repubblica*, with reporter Natalia Aspesi, he admitted with (false?) modesty: "I have nothing momentous to say, I love only my work and I adapt like a chameleon to the needs of the market: Fendi must project an image of a modern and dynamic Italy, and offers me the precious collaboration of Silvio, a talent from the Fendi family, Chanel that of the eternally supreme elegance of the French."

102 From behind the curtain, Karl Lagerfeld observes the reaction of guests at his first show at Patou; it is the 1959 Fall/Winter collection.

103 Having become artistic director of Maison Patou in 1958, the young Lagerfeld designed his creations under the name Roland Karl.

In 1983, Karl Lagerfeld was called in to improve the lot of the House of Chanel. "When I began working there," he related in an interview with CNN, "it wasn't in the least trendy. The owner told me: I'm not satisfied with how things are going. If you can do something, good. Otherwise, I will sell." Lagerfeld succeeded in doing something. He was not scared of criticism. He dared. Little by little he rejuvenated the house's image. He updated its rules. He transformed the double-C into an global icon, the white camellia into a symbol of luxury and elegance, the little black jacket into a universal fetish, Mademoiselle Coco's 2.55 into the most imitated and desirable handbag in the world. In Lagerfeld's hands, Bouclé wool, the label fabric of Coco Chanel and iconic textile of the 1950s, became an intricate weave of precious fibers, sequins, and feathers. The suit made a comeback, and was transformed, from season to season, with changes to proportion, material, and color. La *petite veste* (the Chanel jacket) was reinvented, worn with a mini- or knee-length skirt, with colored suits, with jeans, and was embroidered or came in pastel or glowing hues, or in black and white.

The pearls, the bijoux, the chains, the two-tone shoes, all the elements representing the quintessence of the Chanel style, came back into fashion, new but recognizable, and what counted more, they were even more desirable. Thanks to Kaiser Karl, the label reasserted its supremacy in fashion and luxury goods.

104 The iconic elements of the House of Chanel enjoyed a revival thanks to the creativity of "Kaiser Karl;" among these the suit, presented here in the 2001-2002 Fall/Winter collection.

105 Sunglasses and white hair pulled back in a ponytail make up his "signature style," the elements that make him a universally recognizable iconic figure.

A creative and unstoppable couturier ("I am a sort of fashion nymphomaniac who never achieves orgasm."), Lagerfeld is not satisfied with the successes that have punctuated his fashion career, and is also a photographer, costume-designer, film maker, a creator of advertising campaigns for brands for which he, not exclusively, designs, creates costumes for opera, has designed a bottle for Coca Cola Light and a commercial for Algida Ice Cream...and so on.

Eclectic and visionary, the indisputable Kaiser of fashion is highly proficient in capturing zeitgeist and transforming it into a consumer product. His passion for the 18th century does not prevent him from being an attentive observer of the present one. Lagerfeld seizes, anticipates, and translates today's trends. He designed a line—the first of a long series of celebrated designers to do so—for the low-cost colossus H&M. In love with technology, he shares his thoughts on Twitter. He has gathered millions of followers on Instagram. He has transformed his darling Siamese Choupette into the "world's most famous cat" in order to dedicate a line of inspired accessories to her.

Karl, better than anyone else, creates dreams, ephemera, perhaps, but wonderful precisely for that reason—"My only task is to create desire for that which is not necessary."

106 "A living label," as even Lagerfeld defines himself. In 2010 (and then again in 2011) Lagerfeld lent his face and unmistakable silhouette to a bottle of Coca-Cola Light.

107 A long silk evening gown in black tulle on the runway of a Chanel 2004-2005 Fall/Winter collection.

108 A sample in midnight blue chiffon from the 2009-2010 Fall/ Winter collection presented at the Grand Palais in Paris.

109 Another evening gown from the same collection. Black and white, like camellias, are recurring motifs in Chanel products and continuously reinvented by the designer's talent.

110 The ever-present black leather fingerless gloves are part of Karl Lagerfeld's uniform.

111 Reinterpreted for Chanel women, the same gloves in a silver metallic version were offered as an haute couture accessory in the 2010 Spring/Summer collection. To be paired with a timeless bouclé wool suit.

112 The final item presented on the runway during the 2011-2012 Fall/Winter collection was entitled "Les Allures de Chanel" and was a long white gown with a train.

113 The outfits of Chanel are sartorial masterpieces that require hundreds of hours of labor on the part of tailors and embroideresses capable of translating Karl Lagerfeld's imagination into reality. This fabulous white dress was part of the 2012-2013 Fall/Winter collection.

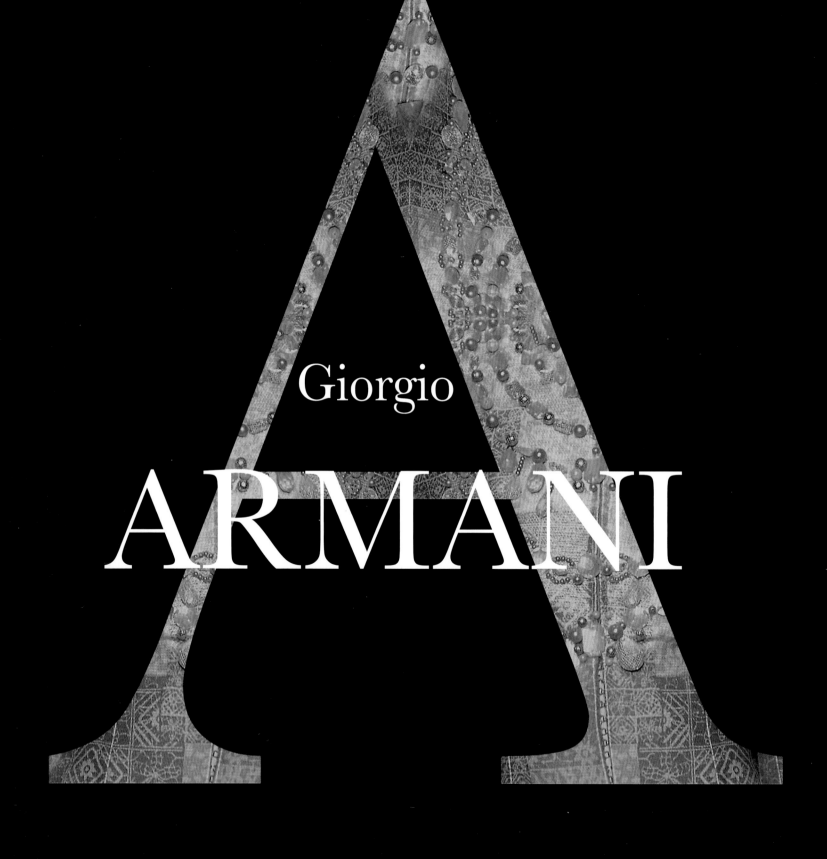

Giorgio **ARMANI**

"AN ARMANI OUTFIT LEAVES NO DOUBTS OR UNCERTAINTIES.
IT'S AN ARMANI, AND THAT IS ALL IT NEEDS TO BE."—SOPHIA LOREN

FEW NAMES IN FASHION EVOKE AS PRECISE AN IMAGE OF STYLE AS GIORGIO ARMANI.

In the almost forty years since the birth of his label, Re Giorgio (King George), as the Italian press nicknamed him, became convinced that "elegance does not mean being noticed, but rather being remembered," and had established not merely a brand but a lifestyle. Simplicity, timeless elegance, and a hushed sensuality, are his coordinates, the same ones that have given life to the chief emblematic item of his House—the jacket, for him and for her, in a back-and-forth series between male and female—and to a love for the world of 'Made in Italy,' which, thanks to Armani, has become synonymous with elegance and quality since the 1970s.

Giorgio Armani was born in Piacenza, on July 11, 1934. Interrupting medical school, and after national service in the army, he worked, in the early 1960s, as a sales clerk and window dresser for the *La Rinascente* department store in Milan, where he began his fashion career in the prêt-à-porter field, working his way up, and acquiring a wealth of experience that helped make him the meticulous and perfectionist entrepreneur that he remains to this day. Realizing his talent, Nino Cerruti asked him to redesign the Hitman brand. It was here that he learned the rigor of men's tailoring and perfected his knowledge of textiles. In order to mass produce a product line that was not qualitatively inferior to high fashion, Armani began to strip classic attire of its superfluous tacking and seams. Thus began the process that led to the birth of the famous "Armani jacket."

The 1970s arrived and Giorgio Armani allowed himself to be convinced by his friend Sergio Galeotti to break into the field. Together they opened a consulting office on Corso Venezia, in Milan, where the two sold, rather than produced, ideas that were easy to mass produce without compromising features of quality tailoring. Giorgio continued his work of stripping away; he eliminated padding and interlining, shifted buttons around, modified shoulder straps, lengthened or shortened collars, and used ever lighter and unconventional fabrics, such as linen, for menswear.

1974 was the year of his first menswear signature collection (and also of the first unstructured men's jacket), followed the next year by one for women. Their success was such that Armani and his partner founded Giorgio Armani Spa. Thus, a great season of ready-to-wear high fashion began with a prêt-à-porter line created by a designer who was to make Milan one of the most important international capitals of fashion.

An Armani jacket gives the wearer a look of the beautiful and the damned à la *American Gigolo* (1980), a movie, starring Richard Gere, which canonized the label's popularity. Sales soared as did the designer's fame. In the 1980s an Armani outfit was a veritable status symbol marking economic success. *Time* magazine devoted a cover to him (an honor previously conceded only to Christian Dior). Above the sun-tanned and smiling face of the charming blue-eyed Italian, was the glowing headline: "Giorgio's Gorgeous Style." Shortly afterwards, in 1982, the reporter Jay Cocks noted: "If clothes are the fabric of history, the texture of time, then this time right now belongs to Armani."

116 A young Giorgio Armani poses with a model wearing a long, silk evening gown.

117 Masculine and feminine are fused in a pantsuit in the Emporio Armani 2014-2015 Fall/Winter collection. An oversized bowler hat completes the look.

GORGEOUS STYLE

With wearability as soft and relaxed as that of human skin, and created from fabrics pilfered from menswear, the jacket immediately appeared as a supporting feature in the female wardrobe. In tweed, and with a highly masculine cut, it was worn, in 1976, with a plissé skirt, became more sophisticated in 1977, and was even worn over a swimsuit in 1978. In the 1980s, the tapered line, with broad shoulders, paired with slacks, gave birth to the pants suit, the "uniform" of career women around the world. Then came the blazer, the Andes-style caban, the kimono, and the tailcoat. In 1992, the tuxedo, feminized through fabric and details, made its appearance on the stage. In the late 1990s, the jacket reasserted itself as a staple, thoroughly emancipated from the suit, and as something to be paired with any item of a woman's closet: a long dress, slacks, or a skirt.

Inspired by the cinema of the 1920s and 1930s, Giorgio Armani created a new Greta Garbo look, simultaneously androgynous and sensual. Evening gowns were not absent from his collections either, and, for the first time, in 1986, they, accompanied by bejeweled purses like the clutch, outsold daywear. Armani, who was soon to become a sought-after designer for celebrities, opened his first store on Rodeo Drive, Beverly Hills. Screen icons Julia Roberts, Michelle Pfeiffer, and Jodie Foster were among the first to place themselves in his hands to ensure that they made a unique and unforgettable appearance at the Oscars.

From the outset, the palette of Armani's collections was composed of neutral tones such as blue, black, grey, and brown; in 1997 it was rounded out with 'greige,' a hue between grey and sand. On the runway, Armani exudes a whiff of the East. Inspiration comes from the Arab world, from the culture of Japan and China, influencing above all his high fashion line, *Armani Privé*, established in 2005.

Today, Giorgio Armani is an empire extending from Milan to Hong Kong. King George, president and CEO of the diversified group, is still at its head. With its ten lines (Emporio Armani emerged in 1981, predating by many years the proliferation of a secondary line), the label covers the entire spectrum of today's lifestyles with its signature apparel, accessories, cosmetics, furnishings, flowers, chocolates, and even a chain of hotels and resorts.

As the ageless Armani women entered the new millennium, with the grace, elegance and charm that always set them apart, one may ask "What are the secrets of this master of minimalism and elegance?" The only answer is this: he knows how to grasp the needs, and desires, of his time and turn them into timeless apparel.

119 An item from Armani Privé 2011-2012 Fall/Winter collection. The embroidered cherry blossoms are the designer's tribute to Japan.

120 and 121 Inspiration for the Armani Privé 2008 Spring/Summer collection, once again, comes from the Orient. This time, the India of the maharajah influenced the rich bejeweled ornaments and precious embroideries.

122 The jacket, deconstructed and soft, is a basic feature of the Armani woman's wardrobe, as in this example, part of the prêt-à-porter Giorgio Armani 2014 Spring/Summer collection.

123 Grey, in all its many shades, is one of the favorite colors of Giorgio Armani, the inventor of 'greige,' a tone between grey and beige.

124 A detail of a sample in the Armani Privé 2011 Spring/Summer collection, inspired, as the designer states, by the glitter of precious stones.

125 A fluttering cape, in blue silk, makes its appearance in the 2014 Spring/Summer collection.

126 An exquisite, high-fashion evening gown from the Armani Privé 2012-2013 Fall/Winter collection.

127 In January, 2005, Giorgio Armani celebrated his seventieth birthday and the thirtieth anniversary of his House with a fabulous show of his 2005 Spring/Summer collection.

Yves
SAINT LAURENT

"I BELIEVE THAT I HAVE NEVER BETRAYED THE BOY WHO SHOWED HIS SKETCHES WITH GREAT TREPIDATION TO CHRISTIAN DIOR."

"I have lived for this profession, I have always loved and respected it through and through; fashion is not an art but it needs an artist to exist; apparel is certainly less important than music, architecture, painting, but it was what I knew how to do and what I did, participating in the transformations of my era." It was January 2002. A sense of massive commotion pervaded the runway at the Pompidou Center in Paris. Yves Saint Laurent was bidding farewell to the fashion world with an incredible retrospective show, starring 300 models. Catherine Deneuve sang "*Ma plus belle histoire d'amour c'est vous*," for her friend.

Born to a well-to-do French family in Oran, then French, Algeria, in 1936, Yves Saint Laurent received his training at the Parisian School of Dior. At the master's death, in 1957, the designer, barely 21 years old, assumed the reins of the House. It was the year of his "Trapèze" collection, and one which designated him the child prodigy of French fashion, and the natural heir of Christian Dior. With its narrow shoulders and full skirts, the Trapeze line was revolutionary, in comparison to the tapered waists and bustiers of the time. The young Yves' collaboration with the House of Dior lasted until 1960, when he was called up for military service. The following year, Yves Saint Laurent, together with his partner and life-long companion, Pierre Bergé, founded his label.

On January 29, 1962, in the studio on Rue Spontini, Yves Saint Laurent presented his first signature collection. The legend had begun. After the international press noted the impeccable cut of his suits, the only ones able to rival those of Chanel, all upper-class women in France wanted to dress in Yves Saint Laurent, while American department stores raced to buy up his patterns. With collection after collection, the young designer revolutionized the concept of feminine elegance with a deep understanding of the demands of women of that time. Those were the years of the sexual revolution. Saint Laurent dressed his women with typically masculine items that simultaneously exalted their femininity. Blouses, blazers, pant suits, bush jackets, and trenchcoats, assumed their place in women's wardrobes.

"The Tuxedo", the symbol of the label, arrived in 1966. As a woman's suit that replaced the evening gown, the tuxedo became the symbol of women's liberation, without failing to provoke scandal.

It was in 1966 that Nan Kemper, a wealthy New York socialite, entered a restaurant in Manhattan wearing a woman's tuxedo. Informed of a prohibition on women dining in slacks, Kemper slipped them off and sat down at a table, wearing only the jacket, the length of a mini-dress. That was a tuxedo by Yves Saint Laurent. Worn with high heels, and, later, also over a bare chest or t-shirt, the tuxedo became the passport for all the young women who were fighting for their rights in that era.

130 Yves Saint Laurent, new artistic designer of the Maison Dior after the Master's death, working on some paper patterns in November 15, 1957.

131 Trained at Christian Dior's school, the designer was barely 21 when he took the reins of the House, in 1957. Here, he poses with his models for the Dior 1957 Spring/Summer collection.

Yves
SAINT LAURENT

132 "The Tuxedo," born in 1966, is the icon of Yves Saint Laurent's fashion and of women's emancipation.

133 A couture item with black lace down the back, designed by Yves Saint Laurent. The designer presented his first signature collection on January 29, 1962, in his atelier on Rue Spontini.

That was a period of great cultural ferment, rich in glamor and sensuality, with no barriers or limits, night clubs and heavy drug usage. Yves and his circle of chic friends were photographed by paparazzi at Régine and Club Sept in Paris. The designer's muses—Betty Catroux, Loulou de la Falaise, and Paloma Picasso—beautiful, in unconventional ways, and bold in spirit and style—were far removed from the female models that had inspired Christian Dior.

Expressions of that same provocative beauty that knew no rules, of that desire for liberty, and that discovery of a world that took part in the spirit of the times, were creations inspired by art and by exotic voyages to Russia, China, Spain, Japan, Africa, and Morocco.

The celebrated *Mondrian Robe*, sartorial tribute to the Dutch painter Piet Mondrian, the collections inspired by the works of Matisse, the paintings of Picasso, Andy Warhol's Pop Art, the writings of Proust, the Russian ballet, and, later, the *Bambara* dresses worn by colored models, as if by so many African princesses, the Safari look, the Chinese, Moroccan, and Indian collections, were the means by which Yves Saint Laurent spread his wandering gaze across the world, bringing art, culture, and exoticism to the runway.

His creations—though far from mundane—introduced a more democratic idea of luxury, far from the rigidity and conventions of couture.

Yves Saint Laurent was the first couturier to create a prêt-à-porter line destined to be not simply a cheaper version of high fashion, sold at the back of an atelier, as was the case with Madeleine Vionnet and Lucien Lelong in the 1920s and 1930s, but a line with a clear creative identity. *Yves Saint Laurent Rive Gauche* was created in 1966.

In the 1970s, Yves Saint Laurent and Pierre Bergé were ruling an empire. The gilded letters YSL stood out on every item, from perfume to shower curtains. Yves Saint Laurent was so famous that he turned himself into the ideal testimonial of his own label. In 1971 he posed naked, wearing only his eyeglasses, in an advertisement for the men's fragrance *Pour Homme*. He was the first designer to use his own face to promote one of his products.

In 1980, his output was so prolific and significant that the Metropolitan Museum in New York devoted a retrospective to him. But dependence on drugs, and depression, had an impact on the designer's creative streak. The talented pencil of the child prodigy of French fashion ceased to innovate and limited itself to revisiting his iconic pieces of the past. When the brand was acquired by the Gucci group, the prêt-à-porter line was assigned to Tom Ford; Yves continued to place his name on high-end fashion until 2002, the year in which YSL Haute Couture finally ended operations.

134 The 1965 Mondrian collection, inspired by
the Dutch painter, captures the trends of that time,
characterized by clean horizontal and vertical lines,
and boxy garments.

134-135 Dreams of the future influenced the fashion
of the 1960s. Models, with their futuristic headdresses,
seem to have landed on Yves Saint Laurent's runway.

136 A smiling Katoucha poses in her "guitar" dress, part of the 1988 Cubist collection.

137 left "Les yeux d'Elsa" ["Elsa's eyes"], a jacket designed by Yves Saint Laurent for the 1988 Spring/ Summer collection, reappeared on the runway during a show held in January 2002—a retrospective of the designer's most beautiful creations—which marked his retirement from the scene after a 40-year career.

137 right A sketch of one of the designer's evening gowns.

138 A pattern designed for the 2006-2007 Fall/ Winter collection by Stefano Pilati, artistic director of Yves Saint Laurent between 2004 and 2012.

139 The iconic bow dress of 1983—which became emblematic of Yves Saint Laurent designs' signature femininity thanks to its sinuous silhouette and enormous pink bow at the back—returns to the runway during the designer's farewell show at the Pompidou Center, in Paris, in January 2002.

140 Katoucha posing in a magnificent cape covered with pheasant and vulture feathers.

141 On January 22, 2002, in an emotionally charged setting, Yves Saint Laurent bade farewell to the fashion world with an incredible retrospective show that brought together 300 models. Next to the designer and his friend are Laetitia Casta and Catherine Deneuve—dressed in the 1966 tuxedos that became leitmotifs for the label.

" ...today I have decided to bid farewell to that profession that I have loved so well."
YSL

After a long illness, Yves Saint Laurent passed away, at the age of 71, in early June, 2008. The designer's body was cremated and his ashes scattered in Le Jardin Marjorelle, the garden of his villa in Marrakesh.

Stefano Pilati succeeded Tom Ford; then, with the arrival of Hedi Slimane as artistic director, in 2012, the brand changed its name to Saint Laurent Paris. "Yves" was deleted from the label, but not from memory. Yves Saint Laurent made a profound mark on the history of apparel, accompanying women of the last century in their great move toward liberation and creating the wardrobe of the contemporary woman.

If Coco Chanel had liberated women, Yves Saint Laurent had given them power, permitting them to express femininity and seduction with an androgynous fashion that drew on men's closets. These were new women, courageous and sensually powerful.

Ralph

LAUREN

"EVERYTHING IS POSSIBLE. I AM LIVING PROOF OF THAT."

HIS REAL NAME IS NOT LAUREN, BUT LIFSHITZ. HE DID NOT GROW UP IN AN ANCIENT ENGLISH MANOR HOUSE BUT IN THE BRONX. HE DID NOT PLAY POLO, YET POLO INSPIRED THE LOGO OF HIS BRAND. HE HAD NEVER YET BEEN ON AN AFRICAN SAFARI WHEN HE BEGAN DESIGNING GORGEOUS APPAREL IN KHAKI.

There is a great deal of imagination in the history of Ralph Lauren. There is the belief that clothing helps transform the person who wears it into what he or she wishes to be, and that everything in life can be achieved through talent and determination. In a short word, the American dream.

"Everything is possible, I am living proof of that," the designer maintains with pride. From the outset, Ralph Lauren—the American self-made man incarnate—drew from the world to which he did not belong by birth but which he conquered through his own labors.

Classic, tailored, and elegant, Ralph Lauren's look is directed a little toward Old England and a little toward the WASP aesthetic of America's social elite, which devotes itself to the aristocratic sports of tennis, yachting and polo—precisely those that are most glamorous, sexy and international.

A cowboy, an English lord, the leading character in a black-and-white movie: all these are figments of the designer's imagination. His inspiration is a romantic history of stars and stripes that encompasses the western, the glamour of the Old Hollywood of the 1920s and 1930s, and the novels of F. Scott Fitzgerald. It was not by accident that he was chosen to design Robert Redford's costumes for *The Great Gatsby* (1974). F. Scott Fitzgerald's character, Jay Gatsby, is one to whom Ralph Lauren is often compared in terms of ambition and self-invention.

Ralph Lifshitz was born in the Bronx, to a poor family of Jewish immigrants. Between 1956 and 1966 he worked, on commission, for various department stores in New York City, including Bloomingdale's. In the meantime he attended a series of business management courses at City College in New York. In 1967 he designed a collection of ties with the label 'Polo.' Its success was such that the following year he launched a line of menswear. Thus emerged 'Polo by Ralph Lauren.'

There followed Oxford shirts, cashmere crew-sweaters and a blazer—Ralph Lauren created a traditional male wardrobe inspired by the past. He designed, for himself, what he liked to wear but created a style—soon regarded as typically American—that pleased the entire world.

His affair with women's apparel began when he started designing outfits for his wife Ricky. It was for her that he adapted men's clothing items. He entered the prêt-à-porter of women's fashion in 1971, with a shirt collection. Ralph Lauren's women assumed the Annie Hall look (in the Woody Allen film, Diane Keaton drew on her personal wardrobe, which included a signature Ralph Lauren jacket and tie), and dressed in tweed, country chic style.

145 A backstage photo of the Ralph Lauren show of September 13, 2012, during the Mercedes-Benz Fashion Week in New York. For this collection, the designer drew elements from Spanish and Latin-

That same year he launched his famous men's polo shirt (with the logo of the polo player on horseback) which came in 24 colors and became a must-have item in the preppy style so much in vogue in the 1990s.

With collection after collection, the designer covered the history of the United States. The *Santa Fe* collection (1981) was full of Navajo-inspired motifs and prints, cowboy belts, voluminous petticoats, and roomy, blanket-like overcoats. This was followed by other collections inspired by the Far West, the pilot, Amelia Earhart, and folksy Americana, and through which Lauren captured the essence of American culture, intertwining the Polo brand with the history of his country.

His captivating publicity campaigns, designed by Bruce Weber, have, likewise, been infused with patriotism. The same can be said of the designer's involvement in major sports events—above all the Olympic games, for which he has created many of the US uniforms—as was his gift of 13 million dollars to restore the "star-spangled banner," the first flag of the United States, in 1998.

The boy who did not follow fashion, but who was "observing women" with the objective to "realize the dream of dreams: a reality more beautiful than anyone could imagine," is today the head of a global empire quoted on Wall Street and one of the 200 richest individuals in the world on the *Forbes* list. Nevertheless, he still continues to pursue the American dream, its spirit of freedom, nature, and unlimited territory. A timeless legacy that affects, and still succeeds, in influencing all of his creations.

146 A model wearing a pinstripe suit inspired by menswear, along with a tie and a beret, from the 2010 Spring/Summer collection.

147 The Far West has often been the source of imaginative ideas for the designer, the creator of sophisticated contemporary cowgirl outfits, such as this one in the 2011 Spring/Summer collection.

148 The Ralph Lauren woman, presented in the 2013 Spring/Summer collection, dressed in a richly decorated matador's jacket and long silk dress, inspired by the costumes of flamenco dancers.

149 The opulence of toreador costumes was reinterpreted by the designer in these pants adorned with gold embroidery.

Vivienne

WESTWOOD

THERE ARE FEW DESIGNERS TO WHOM CAN BE CONCEDED
THE PRIVILEGE OF A FORMAL MEETING WITH HER MAJESTY,
THE QUEEN. EVEN FEWER INVESTED WITH AN OBE,
AND, LATER A DBE.

Only one, however, who, after receiving her OBE, saluted the photographers at Buckingham Palace by executing a bold spin and lifting the full skirt of her military-inspired suit to show the world a certain indifference to underwear. That was in 1992, and no one else but Vivienne Westwood could have afforded this light-hearted—but according to her involuntary—antic, in such circumstances. The show was repeated fourteen years later, when she received her DBE from Prince Charles. When he asked why she held such a grudge against briefs, she replied: "Don't ask. It's the same answer. I don't wear them with dresses. When I'm wearing trousers I might - my husband's silk boxers."

Who else but the designer, who had dressed the Sex Pistols, then at the top of the charts, with their subversive *God Save the Queen*, could have executed such a "scabrous" gesture with such impudent grace? Who else, in short, if not the Queen of provocation, who, if not the *maitresse à penser* of scandal, even in terms of music, who did such things with the ultimate goal of destroying the system at its very roots, who, if not the muse—if not the inventor herself—of the most anarchic and nihilistic juvenile subculture of the times?

And to think that Vivienne Isabel Swire could have led a tranquil—and, all in all, very ordinary—existence as a provincial schoolteacher. Born in Tintwistle, Derbyshire, on April 8, 1941, to a petty bourgeois family, she did not seem destined for an over the top life, so to speak. After moving to the outskirts of London with her family, she began to study art, resigning herself, fairly soon however, to the stability of a career as an elementary schoolteacher. She married young to Derek Westwood, and bore a son. And here her story might have ended, as did other stories of so many possibly repressed, certainly dissatisfied, women had not she crossed paths with music producer Malcolm McLaren, destined to pass into the history of pop culture as the manager of the Sex Pistols, and the "decoder" of punk. Westwood fell in love with him, and as soon as he decided to open a bizarre shop of equally bizarre fashion at No. 430, King's Road, London, she did not think twice about following him with great enthusiasm. *Let it Rock* was to change its name many times in the course of a few years; it became *Too Fast To Live Too Young To Die* in 1972, *Sex* in 1974, then *Seditionaries*, and finally, *World's End*. But its spirit never changed.

152 Vivienne Westwood in 1977, posing on a London street with two other exponents of the punk movement. Leather pants and bomber jackets, studs, safety pins, dyed hair and Mohawks, torn garments and hints of sadomasochism: punk fashion was born to shock.

153 Westwood and her husband, music producer Malcolm McLaren, posing in 1985 in their legendary shop, World's End, at 430 King's Road, London, a beacon for the punk movement.

IT WAS THERE THAT THE SEX PISTOLS FOUND THEIR STAGE COSTUMES, WHICH WERE CREATED EXPRESSLY FOR THEM BY WESTWOOD.

It was there that punks, sporting colored Mohawks, met to replenish their store of t-shirts decorated with zippers, safety pins, even chicken bones spelling out obscene slogans, leather biker jackets, combat boots, chains serving as necklaces, sadomasochistic accessories, and tartan trousers. Their deliberate anti-social activities found an ideal instrument in Vivienne Westwood's outfits, in a head-on, and hard, defiance of the establishment, which will never again in history find a moment of such perfect synthesis of street, fashion, and music. Obscenity, violence, and rebellion were all sublimated in an aesthetic that still has a following today. It did nothing to placate authorities, however, which repeatedly tried to close MacLaren and Westwood's punk hide-out.

When, inevitably, punk too became conformist, Westwood realized that her fashion had to take a more conscious, mature, and in a certain sense, institutional turn. Safety pins and chains were locked away, and lace, crochet, puffed sleeves, high-leg boots and eccentric hats emerged from the designer's imagination, to appear for the first time in fashion shows held in Paris, the mecca of Fashion with a capital F, in March 1981. With her legendary collection Pirate, Vivienne Westwood, the only British woman to have a show in the *City of Light* since Mary Quant, acquired, to all intents and purposes, the status of "true" designer, launching a fashion—New Romanticism—that, once again, intertwined costume and music.

154 Vivienne Westwood adjusts a pirate's hat on the head of Annabella Lwin, singer with Bow Bow Wow, the English New Wave band founded by Malcolm McLaren. The "Pirate Collection" was the first collection designed by the couple for the runway, and was worn not only by Bow Wow Wow, but also by singer Adam Ant later to become a global sensation.

155 Lace, tatting, puffed and pirate sleeves: after punk, Westwood launched New Romanticism, which, once again, was inspired by, and inspired a music movement.

BUT THAT WAS ONLY THE BEGINNING OF THE "SECOND TIME AROUND" FOR THE DESIGNER'S CAREER; EVER MORE PERCEPTIVE AND PROFOUND, HER ICONOGRAPHIC EXPERIMENTS TURNED AWAY FROM THE PECULIARITIES OF URBAN TRIBALISM TOWARDS GALLERIES, MUSEUMS, ETHNOGRAPHIC TREATISES AND HISTORICAL STUDIES OF COSTUMES OF THE 17TH AND 18TH CENTURIES.

The intent was always the same, however, namely, to break down the system and pursue liberty, wherever that led. The designer did that from the inside. In 1982, she designed her *Savage* collection, followed by *Nostalgia of Mud*: the integration of decorative elements, and forms, from various periods and cultures, soon became her trademark. 1983 was the moment of her celebrated *Witches* collection, which combined the language of Keith Haring's New York's artistic avant-garde with prehistoric esotericism, while 1986 witnessed a brush with *Mini Crini*, which reinstated a fashion for Victorian petticoats and corsets that, until then, had seemed destined to remain definitively in oblivion. Dedicated to the most radical eclecticism, Westwood's experiments never seemed, in fact, to abate, and remain alive and vibrant to this day. The same goes for her direct and almost endearing attack on authority: in 1989, she posed for the *Tatler* disguised as, and made up like, Margaret Thatcher, wearing an outfit that the British Prime Minister had commissioned but not yet collected. And who knows if she had not enjoyed a touch of sadistic pleasure in seeing Naomi Campbell, then Queen of global fashion, stumble on the runway, during a show in 1993, while wearing a pair of platform shoes, which were "too" high even for her, top of the top supermodels.

WESTWOOD

158 The fusion of different eras and cultures has always been the unmistakable signature of Vivienne Westwood. As are her ideas on ecology, which she has propagated for many years, through her shows. A model with painted features emerges as a present-day eco-warrior in the 2010 Spring/Summer collection.

159 Vivienne Westwood's Red Label 2013 Spring/ Summer collection concluded with the appearance of the designer wearing a t-shirt brandishing "Climate Revolution," the project she funds, through Greenpeace, which aims to preserve the Arctic.

Always a step ahead of the rest, Westwood has, for some years, been engaged in determined activism in the social, civic, and in her way, political sphere, taking advantage of the visibility offered by, and on, her shows to launch ecological messages and support for nuclear disarmament, and bringing media attention to her new battles of *Active Resistance*. At the same time, with enviable light-heartedness and charming inconsistency, she was able to create every woman's dream white dress, which appeared on the romantic heroine par excellence, Carrie Bradshaw of *Sex and the City*, who, in the movie adaptation of the cult series, did not get married, wearing a Vivienne Westwood creation.

And it is thus that a designer, who set herself the goal of destroying the collective imagination, re-entered it through the schmalziest of fashions.

"... OF COURSE, YOU KNOW ME AS A DESIGNER, BUT I AM, ABOVE ALL,
A PASSIONATE READER AND LOVER OF ART..."

160 The queen of punk, with her models, at the finale of the 2011-2012 Fall/Winter collection. A collection that celebrates the World Wide Woman, that is, the strong contemporary woman and female guardian of culture, values, and naturally, nature. The bride, wrapped by the designer's own hands in meters and meters of white tulle, struts out to the notes of "I Will Survive."

161 The ecological campaign continues in the 2013-2014 Fall/Winter collection, presented by neo-warriors who bear the message "Climate Revolution."

Yohji
YAMAMOTO

"ONE COULD SAY THAT DESIGNING IS VERY EASY:
THE DIFFICULTY LIES IN IDENTIFYING A NEW WAY OF EXPLORING BEAUTY."

A NUCLEAR EXPLOSION.
THUS THE EUROPEAN PRESS DESCRIBED YOHJI YAMAMOTO'S RUNWAY DEBUT IN PARIS,
DUBBING HIS COLLECTION "POST-ATOMIC FASHION."

It was 1981 when the Japanese designer arrived in the French capital, causing a veritable shockwave in the fashion world. Black dresses, rips, asymmetries and visible seams were a revolutionary spectacle for the eyes of European designers. It was the era of Claude Montana's fatal women, Thierry Mugler's uninhibited glamor, Jean-Paul Gaultier's disturbing conical bra. It was an era of bright colors and unscrupulous hedonism which Yamamoto countered with pitch black and refined poverty. An era of exhibitionism and excess in the midst of which he launched a fashion that veiled rather unveiled.

For Yohji Yamamoto, born in 1943, in Tokyo, the marks of the war were indelible, and lived on between the incomplete seams, and the gashes, in the cloth. "Within me the war has never ended; within me there is no post-war," remarked the designer in *Notebooks on Cities and Clothes* (1989), a biographical film by Wim Wenders.

After earning his diploma, from the Bunka Gakuen School of Fashion, Yamamoto exhibited in Tokyo, in 1977, as brand Y's; a few years later he abandoned the Japanese capital for Paris. There, after the shocking debut of 1981, he struck again in 1983 with his *Refined Poverty* collection. The poetic dimension of his creations inaugurated a new school of thought in fashion.

More interested in the process than in the finished product—"I am never happier than at the initial stage of development. From that point on the product is a reality. And reality strikes. My heart pounds throughout the process. Even though the decisive day always arrives."—Yamamoto introduced the concept of deconstruction to Western fashion.

Subverting tradition, he revealed the individual stages of the process of sewing a garment. He disclosed techniques and secrets. Folds and pleats that served to create ornamental motifs, as did frayed hems, basting, collars and buttons, which, when applied in unconventional arrangements, lost their function, while making abstract patterns, and asymmetry, the prevalent criteria.

His ideal item comes in no size. Sometimes it is too small, more often than not it is too large, leaving the body it contains to one's imagination. His is a "destitute and mysterious style that feeds on poor and belabored materials, that subsists on covering, not uncovering, a body, that values intelligence over beauty."

164 A 2005 portrait of the designer, master of refined poverty and deconstruction.

165 A detail from one of the creations in the 2006 Spring/Summer collection. Ropes and industrial piping decorate the evening gowns—more objets d'art than haute couture.

FROM THIS SAME PERSPECTIVE, YAMAMOTO EXPERIMENTS WITH IMPERFECTION, ABSTRACTING ALL THAT IS BROKEN, WITHERED, DIRTY (*HIFU* IN JAPANESE) FROM EVERYTHING AROUND HIM.

He wants "scars, failures, disorder." Thus, the "unfinished" garment respects the emotional frailty of the person who wears it. Asymmetry and mismatched sizes are proofs of our imperfection in as much as we are human. If symmetry is not human, neither are high heels, which he replaced by flats, nor are jewels or any type of ornament, which he bans from his aesthetic. His products are odes to darkness.

Black is the dominant color. Over the years, however, his collections have been enhanced by other hues: white, blue, vibrant red, colors in sharp contrast to black. Yamamoto loves school, military, even ecclesiastical uniforms. What fascinates him is their function. Conceived to last a long time, uniforms become part of the identity of the person who wears them. Just like his creations. "A garment of mine is forever," he often repeats, denying the transience of fashion,—at least his fashion. "Buying a new jacket means buying a new life, something that totally changes one's lifestyle. With this I mean to say: please don't make my clothes an object of consumption, they will live with you forever. In fashion, things change every six months, while in my philosophy things don't work this way: you can wear an item for at least ten, twenty years without worrying about novelty." The ideal garment, therefore, does not fall out of fashion. Like a uniform, it becomes part of the identity, and lifestyle, of the person who wears it.

A creator of avant-garde fashion for intellectual, and versatile, men and women of culture, Yamamoto has, over the years, gotten involved in art films, transformed himself into a costume designer for the cult movies of Takeshi Kitano, for theater and dance—outfitted the choreographer and dancer Pina Bausch—and also worked on mass culture phenomena—designing the stage costumes for concerts by Elton John and Placebo. More popular, and accessible, to a vast public are the products of his signature Y-3 label, established in 2003 in collaboration with Adidas. From his building in central Tokyo, maintained by several hundred dependents, and his mother, a seamstress and his first teacher, the standard bearer of Japanese couture, on Paris runways, continues to fascinate the public with his collections of conceptual fashion, for him and for her.

166 The standard-bearer of Japanese couture, shown in his Tokyo atelier in 1995.

167 A long leather overcoat from the 2008-2009 Fall/Winter collection.

168 and 169 Though black is the dominant color of his products, other hues have enriched his collections from time to time. In the 2008 Spring/Summer collection, for example, single hues were interrupted by floral and dragon prints, and gilt leathers.

170 The final item in the 2011 Spring/Summer collection consisted of a yellow skirt seemingly made of an inflatable mattress.

171 A dress from the 2013-2014 Fall/Winter collection envisaged as an origami sculpture.

172 Layers of neon colors sweep through the 2014 Spring/Summer collection, marking an evolution in the fashion of Yamamoto, an avant-garde designer who never tires of experimentation.

173 The 2014-2015 Fall/Winter collection consisted of an enormous, all-encompassing cocoon overcoat. After the traditional black of his early output, Yamamoto surprised us with graffiti-type designs hand painted on feathers.

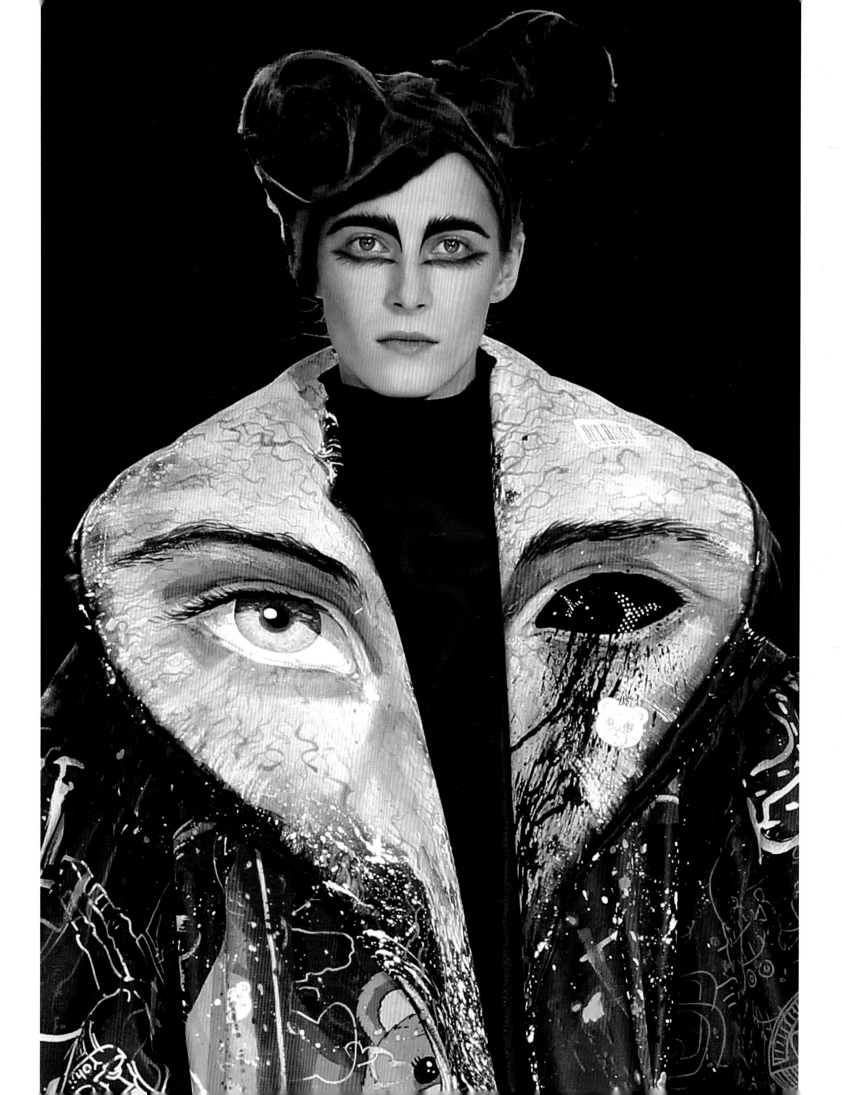

174 A detail of an item in the 2014 Spring/Summer collection described as "Meaningless Excitement," that is, senseless frenzy, in which the designer experimented with new cuts, new superimpositions, and new colors.

175 A touch of irony in gloves displaying manicured nails, part of the 2013-2014 Fall/Winter collection.

Gianfranco FERRÉ

"A FUNDAMENTAL FACTOR THAT LED ME TO FASHION WAS PASSION,
A NEARLY PHYSICAL NEED FOR DIRECT RAPPORT WITH THE MATERIAL OF MY CREATION."

THEY CALL HIM THE ARCHITECT OF FASHION—BOTH BECAUSE HE GRADUATED FROM THE POLYTECHNIC IN MILAN IN 1969, AND, ABOVE ALL, BECAUSE HE CREATED A STYLE BASED ON PRECISE LINES, STRUCTURED GARMENTS AND PERFECT CUTS.

Born in Legnano, Lombardy, in 1944, to a family of small-scale manufacturers, Gianfranco Ferré entered the world of fashion in the early 1970s by creating scarfs and costume jewelry for Walter Albini, raincoats for the Sangiorgio rainwear company in Genoa, and t-shirts for Fiorucci. During this time he would commute, by train, where he met the people who would help him launch his label: Rita Airaghi, a distant cousin, who became his right-hand person in the management of the brand's communications, and Franco Mattioli, an entrepreneur from Bologna, his partner from 1975 to 1999. In 1978, he founded Gianfranco Ferré Spa, with Mattioli, and that same year he presented his first womenswear collection.

It was the beginning of a dazzling career, punctuated by successes in every area of womenswear—from prêt-à-porter to high fashion (he debuted at Alta Roma in 1986), from Milan to Paris (in 1989 he was asked to assume the reins of Dior and remained its head until 1997)—and menswear (his first menswear collection came in 1982). At the end of each of his shows, when the Great Lombard—so called because of his powerful proportions—appeared on the runway, he was greeted with thunderous applause.

His grandiose, yet impeccable fashion caused a stir. Like a sculptor, the designer molded fabrics around the female torso, transforming them into spectacular and surprising creations. In his hands, silk, chiffon, even less expensive materials such as nylon and raffia, became not only gorgeous garments, but an integral part of the body that they enveloped.

The "analytical and logical method that teaches and educates creativity" which he picked up while studying architecture, induced him to pay particular attention to sartorial production—with a nearly maniacal concern for detail. Nevertheless, Ferré used rigorous technique to fulfill his dreams.

From the very onset of his career, he was nostalgic for post-war Italy and the years of *La Dolce Vita* (1960), which he brought back to life through his creations, with a deeply personal and modern touch. Somewhere, between the logic and the dream, lay the emblematic icon of his House: the white shirt filched from a man's closet and transformed into an instrument of seduction. Sometimes light and billowing, sometimes impeccable and severe, sumptuous and beguiling, simple or full of frills and embroidery, "it soared to frame the face. It sculpted the body to transform it into a second skin." "Read with glamor and poetry, with freedom and enthusiasm (...) it revealed that it was gifted with a thousand identities."

178 Gianfranco Ferré backstage during the 1995 Spring/Summer collection, arranges Carla Bruni's hair before she proceeds to the runway.

179 A sample item from the 2004 Spring/Summer prêt-à-porter collection. The structured, almost architectural silhouette, and perfectly tailored cuts, are characteristic of Ferré's style.

Equilibrium, elegance, and sobriety were the stylistic trademarks not only of his products but also of his lifestyle. Gianfranco Ferré did not love high society; he stayed on the margins of show business and returned, as often as he could, to his hideaway home in Legnano, where he concentrated on all his passions: works of art, travel souvenirs, collections of objects purchased at flea-markets, such as the tie clip that became the distinctive symbol (which today we would call the *signature style*) of his personal style.

The designer's unexpected death from a cerebral hemorrhage, in 2007, at the age of 62, shocked the world of fashion. The show that followed it ended with a bird's eye view of pure white shirts, the consistent thread of all his work, and the classic item that the designer had raised to the loftiest peak of refinement and elegance, raising it to a place in its own right in the history of fashion, and in the "contemporary lexicon of elegance," which allowed it to become an "element of universal use, which, however, everyone could interpret in his or her own way." The Swedish designer Lars Nilsson, the Italian designers Tommaso Aquilano and Roberto Rimondi, and, finally, the creative duo Federico Piaggi and Stefano Citron, succeeded one another in holding the reins of the House of Ferré. The terrible news, that Ferré was closing its, doors, came during Milan Fashion Week in February 2014. The decision had been taken by the Paris Group, a company from Dubai that had owned the brand since 2011. Had his successors somehow failed to measure up to the master or was Ferré—once a precursor of fashion and style—no longer sufficiently up to date? Who can say? What is certain is that it was a severe blow to 'Made in Italy' and a grave loss for Italy's cultural heritage. A piece of history—not only in terms of fashion—which needs to be preserved.

180 Helena Christensen in September 2003, wearing a white shirt by Gianfranco Ferré. Reinvented, available in multiple variants, planned with the precision of an architect, the white shirt turns into magic when worn by a top model.

181 The main icon of the designer's gift for planning, the white shirt returns to the stage in a 2004 Spring/Summer collection.

182 Deconstructed, disassembled, and then reassembled, Ferré's iconic white blouse, a recurring theme in his collections, became a dress in October 1991.

183 A dress from 1991 created by the designer for Christian Dior. Ferré was the head of the House between 1989 and 1997, interpreting, with his unique touch, themes dear to the French couturier.

184 A magnificent, intricately embroidered evening gown appeared on the runway during the 2006 Spring/Summer collection.

185 Fur stole and tooled leather corset belt for a strapless dress with a full skirt in neutral earth tones presented in the 2006 Fall/Winter collection.

Gianni
VERSACE

WITHOUT GIANNI THERE WOULD HAVE BEEN NO NAOMI, LINDA, OR CLAUDIA. OR RATHER, WITHOUT THE SEXY, BOLD, INFURIATINGLY FEMININE FASHION OF GIANNI VERSACE THERE WOULD, PROBABLY, NOT HAVE BEEN THAT UNREPEATABLE AND UNFORGETTABLE GOLDEN AGE OF MODERN FASHION, WHICH ENTERED THE HISTORY OF FASHION AS THE ERA OF THE SUPER MODEL.

It was the designer from Calabria, born on December 2, 1946, and who did not become famous, in fact, until the turn of the 1990s, who built up that squad of modern beauty goddesses, of nearly mythological proportions, who came to be known to the general public (and not merely to the restricted elite assigned to the job) solely by their first name, but who, nevertheless, did have surnames: Campbell, Evangelista, and Schiffer. But also Christy Turlington, Cindy Crawford, Helena Christensen, Elle MacPherson, Carla Bruni (more recently known by her married name, perhaps, of Sarkozy), Tatjana Patitz, Stephanie Seymour, and Kate Moss. Not only were these beautiful icons, but their unattainable perfection was immortalized in the works of legendary photographers such as Richard Avedon, Helmut Newton, Steven Meisel, and Irving Penn, whose advertising campaigns of that period are viewed today with the respect granted to veritable works of art. Yet, these were also intelligent women—powerful, brimming with character and personality. And, furthermore, symbols, emblems of a dynamic and disturbing period in recent international fashion, who had the ability to endow fashion itself with the dimension of a dream, grant it an aura of magic, and turn it into a concrete, entertaining, and innocent incarnation of luxury.

And who knows if the young Versace had ever desired, or even imagined as much in his mother's shop at No. 13 via Tommaso Gulli in Reggio Calabria. Perhaps, a lot less would have been enough, for a boy so in love with clothing, for the leap from a dressmaker's studio in the far South to a designer's dazzling atelier is enormous, and even, perhaps, deadly.

Versace made the first of his many leaps at the age of 25, when, like so many in his region, he left behind the cramped quarters of his home, packed his bags, and followed his dreams to Milan, the center of Italian industry, which, more recently, had grown to be the center of fashion. There he began to design for the brands that specialized in nurturing talented youth in search of visibility. It was to Genny and Callaghan, and Complice, which Versace initially sold his imagination and his ingenuity, still naive, simplistic, and superficial, perhaps, but ready to explode in a dazzling display soon afterwards.

On March 28, 1978, the designer presented his first signature collection at the Palazzo della Permanente, in Milan. By this point, his younger sister, Donatella, had already become his muse, a loyal, platinum-haired presence, tirelessly at her brother's side, first as a silent shadow, later as his spiritual heir. His older brother, and business partner, Santo, the company's president and managing director, counter-balanced the artist's volubility with his own pragmatism.

188 Gianni Versace and his sister Donatella in a 1994 portrait: two faces of the same soul, two complimentary figures bound by mutual love and an equal passion for fashion.

189 Theatrical volumes and bold, vibrant colors: femininity, as envisaged by Versace, is palpable, vivid, and practically screaming out at the viewer.

190 A sketch by Gianni Versace. Like a mystery waiting to be unwrapped, his ultra-feminine woman emerges from the unreal vortex of a gown that envelops her.

191 Naomi Campbell, Versace's muse and friend, on the runway, at the unveiling of the label's 1995-1996 Fall/Winter collection. A shower of crystals is all that the black Venus wears.

The designer's highly personal approach immediately became visible on the stage: incomplete at first, but already in full force. The intensity of his expressive power came as a shock because it was precisely what constituted his fashion; it shook and disturbed the canons of tasteful attire, and the security of careful planning, with a sexy and exuberant aesthetic, that "ladies" had never before even thought themselves capable of taking into consideration.

His creations spoke to a self-conscious and open-minded woman, mistress of her own means, and one proud of her seductive powers, at once attractive, but by no means subjugated to her own fragility. In sum, strong in her own alleged vulnerability. The leitmotif of what would become his inimitable style—despite his efforts—could already be read between the lines.

His masterfully skewed, and consciously distorted, view of the history of art and architecture were clear: a passion for classical culture that, nevertheless, permitted a shameless contamination of ancient Greece (which he so loved that he made the mythological figure of Medusa the label's trademark) with the redundant excesses of the baroque, but also the modernity of pop art, in a triumph of a potentially schizophrenic decorative art bordering on, but never quite descending to, the level of kitsch. The most disparate materials were juxtaposed with usual liberty; the gaudiest colors forcibly paired. Classic sartorial techniques, starting with draping, reinvented with constant curiosity and ever-increasing interest in the spectacular.

Making its triumphal appearance on the runway was metal mesh, the futuristic metallic knit that was to become one of the House's unique "must-haves", after 1981, and the introduction of punk and rock culture, that was to reach its peak in one of the most iconic outfits of the past century, a black dress "held-together" by dozens of large golden safety pins, as worn by Elizabeth Hurley on Hugh Grant's arm, in 1994.

ALTHOUGH THE VERSACE STYLE, WITH ITS WONDERFUL BALANCE OF SENSUALITY
AND SEXUALITY, FINDS FERTILE SOIL AMONG CAPRICIOUS AND OUTLANDISH POP STARS,
FROM MADONNA TO ELTON JOHN, IT IS EQUALLY TRUE THAT HIS FASHION, AND IN THIS
LIES ITS POWER, DOES NOT REMAIN RELEGATED TO THE INVARIABLY NARROW CONFINES
OF "SHOCK." YES, VERSACE DID MIX STYLES, BUT WHAT PERHAPS AMUSED HIM MORE WAS
MOCKING THE RULES OF CLASS AND GENRES.

When Lady Diana wished to shake off the cliché of the courtly, clumsy duckling and transform herself into the marvelous swan of newscasts, it was Versace whom she asked to dress her. Yet Gianni's most colorful fantasies did not find their natural home only on stages, hosting the mega concerts of popular music stars, but also on those in famous theaters—not least of which was Milan's La Scala—for which he designed costumes for classical ballet productions, including legendary ones choreographed by his friend Maurice Béjart.

A career, in short, which often grappled with a charge of vulgarity, but which always emerged triumphant, and which had to overcome more than one prejudice. But a career, too, that ended tragically, and prematurely, in Miami Beach on July 15, 1997, entangled in the impersonal and morbid chill of a tale of crime, when the designer was gunned down on the stairway of his luxury villa, Casa Casuarina, by two shots from a pistol fired by serial killer Andrew Cunanan. As newspapers spilled a great deal of ink in reconstructing, analyzing, and making the most of the fantastic speculation, Donatella displayed character, courage and pride. Assuming the role of the label's creative director, she placed herself at the head of the empire he had created. Although perhaps vacillating for a while, it did not collapse, for, as the director Franco Zeffirelli maintained, "with the death of Versace, Italy and the world lost the designer that had freed the world of conformity, and granted it fantasy and creativity," and creativity and fantasy do not die once one has enjoyed a taste of them.

192 A taste for Baroque excess characterizes this red, richly embroidered, evening dress.

193 Another Gianni Versace sketch, from 1989. Color and geometry, borrowed from the 20th-century avant-garde, are fused in a dress dominated by overabundance.

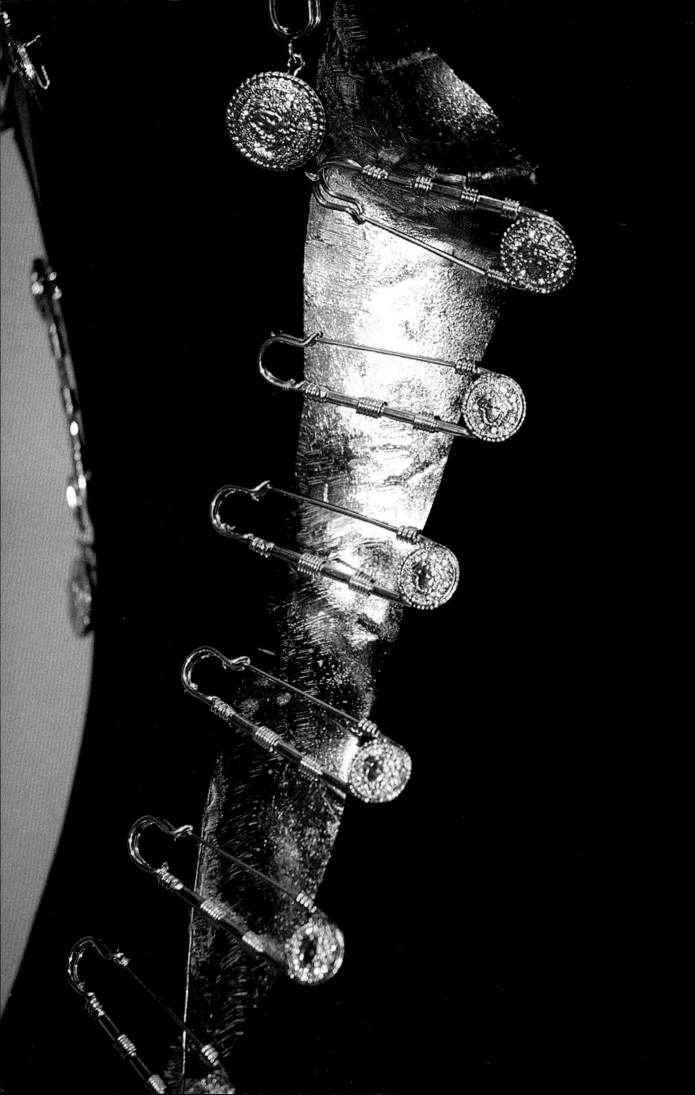

194 A detail from the cult gown worn by actress Elizabeth Hurley during one of her public appearances with ex-partner Hugh Grant. The gold safety pins, that miraculously "hold together" the dress's seams, made 20th-century fashion history.

195 Gold, embroidery, and animal prints: elite model Christy Turlington, on the runway of the 1992 Spring/Summer collection, is decked out in every symbol of femininity. A sexy, modern gypsy, she is the typical embodiment of "Versace style."

Miuccia

PRADA

ONE COULD GET BORED TO DEATH GUESSING THE ROLE THAT DESTINY SEEMED TO HAVE WRITTEN FOR HER, ONE OF THOSE TYPICAL, SOMEWHAT SNOBBISH BOURGEOIS WOMEN FROM MILAN.

If physiognomy bore a grain of truth, she had, a little, in fact, of that air and attitude. But it did not turn out that way. "I always wanted to stand out, I always wanted to be number one," she claimed. Miuccia Prada decided to be a guru of contemporary fashion, a point of reference, an undisputed player. It mattered little that she, herself, pretended to place everything in perspective, declaring "I love clothes. Perhaps I can say that I do not love fashion, but I really love clothes." This is not true: more than the creations of anyone else, hers convey a sense of an aesthetic, social, and, often, even a political viewpoint.

Whether or not one places her on a pedestal, or dares to call her into question, no one can deny the pre-eminence that the elegant Milanese Signora enjoys in today's fashion world. The authoritative magazines *Time* and *Forbes* confirm this in black and white, rightfully including her within the category of the wealthiest businesswomen, and most influential people, in the world.

Prada is, in fact, one of the very few labels that "set" fashion and "dictate" trends. Her shows can be loved by those who understand, or pretend to understand, them, or make those who are not ready to do so, sneer. But what is certain is that the seeds that Prada sows in the fertile soil of fashion, produce a bounteous harvest, the next season, for others. Once her bright idea becomes the norm, she is already contemplating another, ready to give another tug at the unwritten norms of good taste.

That her trajectory was not the easiest, or most predictable, we will see in a second. Born in Milan as Maria Bianchi Prada, in 1949, Miuccia, as she is familiarly known, who frequented the circles of the communist party in her youth, received her diploma in Political Science and took part in—if not in a violent way then at least a heated one—feminist battles that were changing the social structure of Italy in those times. She earned the appellation "aristocommunist" because she did not wish to give up her Yves Saint Laurent and André Courrèges clothing. For five years she attended a course in mime at Giorgio Strehler's Piccolo Teatro in order not to be forced to speak, as she—who would love to have us believe even today that she has never gotten rid of her proverbial timidity—has related. In short, minor or major acts of rebellion that we can imagine her family, perfectly integrated in the social fabric of the high bourgeoisie of Milan, could not have easily digested.

Prada was founded in 1913 by Mario Prada, who opened a shop in the Galleria Vittorio Emanuele II, Milan's high-end shopping center, from which he sold suitcases, trunks, luxury travel goods and silver, horn, and crystal accessories from all over the world, and destined for the most chic homes in Italy, including the royal household, to which he became an official supplier in 1919.

199 An item from the 2010 pre-Fall Miu Miu collection, the second line, launched in 1993, a label that has developed its own clear identity over the course of time.

It was in 1978 that Miuccia, the youngest of Mario's grandchildren, was nearly flung into the directorship of the family business. Her mission was overt and bold: to reinvent the company, rejuvenate it, transform it into a phenomenal success, and turn it into a territory for experimentation and the avant-garde. Her first sensational, and universal success, came in 1985 and took the shape of a series of simple, practically featureless bags and backpacks in black nylon, of the kind used by the army. There was a contradiction, between the handcrafted luxury items for which Prada had become famous, and the somewhat tacky ostentation of the label and logo that had made its fortune in Italy's fashion industry, in the glorious 1980s. Miuccia's black backpacks were a hit, and were sold by the hundreds of thousands because they were able to tap, and perfectly interpret, the new "needs" of the most demanding and knowledgeable fashion victims: functionality, polish, and practicality.

Prada paved the road, even in Italy, for clean, minimal fashion without useless frills. A road that followed a logic, looping around a series of successes, one after the other, with a little help from an alliance—sealed by marriage—with the Tuscan businessman Patrizio Bertelli: in 1988, the debut of women's apparel, in 1993, the launch of the second line Miu Miu, in 1994, the debut of menswear.

Notwithstanding some bold, and occasionally unfortunate, financial operations that led Prada first to buy, then to sell a series of labels such as Fendi, Helmut Lang and Jil Sander, as well as diversified interests, ranging from sports—the adventures of the vessel Luna Rossa in the Americas Cup—to contemporary art, with the creation of a highly active foundation in 1995, Miuccia Prada's approach to creativity has not changed a bit, but, instead, has become even more radical, if possible. As her own muse, and an icon of herself, the designer continues to design exclusively that which she feels like wearing.

She has invented a new sensuality that does not cultivate slit skirts and deep plunging necklines, but combines different elements with nerve, experiments with incompatible materials, and does not surrender, at all, to the limits of common sense and good taste. Flirting with eccentricity, she wheedles out charm from inconsistency. Jumping into the recent history of costume, seizing ideas from here and there, she gives life to never before seen or imagined stylistic Frankenstein monsters. She creates what she likes, but also tries to understand, with a keen and critical eye, what will please the masses. The confused and inorganic amorphous aesthetic universe, consumed by modern society, is absorbed and revised by the designer, who endows it with an ever more cryptic, mysterious, and allusive interpretation. Her creations have cultural and sociological value, or at least this is what the specialized press—as ready as a good semiologist to decipher all the signs that Miuccia disseminates throughout her collections—wants to believe, like the prophecies of the Cumaean Sibyl on palm leaves, entrusted to the capricious wind.

201 An article published in the July 2013 issue of *Madame Figaro* displayed an overcoat, with white and pink Vichy checks, designed by Prada.

202 Miuccia Prada looked to the Orient for the 2013 Spring/Summer collection. The shoes, in particular, are a reinterpretation of Jika Tabi, traditional Japanese footwear.

203 "A perfectly realized powerful idea," thus commented Suzy Menkes, in the *Herald Tribune*, about Prada's 2011 Spring/Summer collection, a baroque musical inspired by a Latin-American beat.

204 A model poses in a Prada dress for the pages of *Madame Figaro*. With its lady-like silhouette, the garment is part of the exclusive 2012-2013 Fall/Winter collection created by the Italian designer for the French department store, Le Printemps.

205 A silver, satin kimono-cloak with floral appliqué, part of the 2013 Spring/Summer collection.

206 Prada's Geisha wearing a glam version of satin Geta sandals with a flat bow and Tabi socks in the 2013 Spring/Summer collection.

207 Fur, even in the summer, for Prada who proposes a stole and a bag with a bold cherry-blossom print.

208 If, in the third millennium, the bond between fashion and art is getting increasingly stronger, this too (and especially) is the work of Miuccia Prada. The 2014 Spring/Summer collection is a clear example of this: the celebration of graffiti art.

209 The impressive murals that serve as a backdrop to the 2014 Spring/Summer collection are the works of artists Miles "El Mac" Gregor, Mesa, Gabriel Specter, Stinkfish, Pierre Mornet and Jeanne Detallante, the last of whom painted the face in the background.

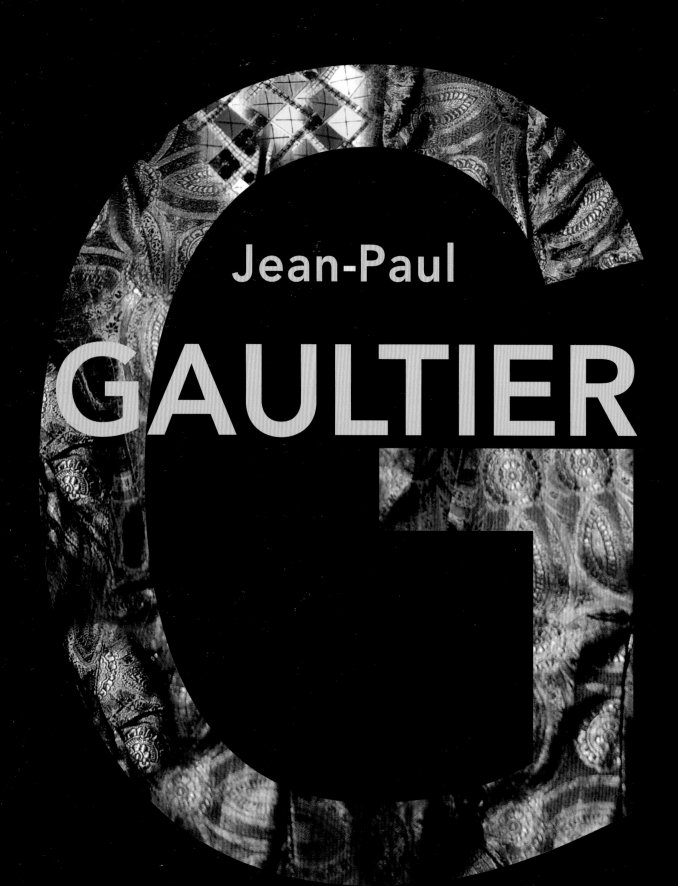

“… WHEN I WAS ASKED, AS A CHILD, WHAT I WANTED TO BE WHEN I GREW UP,
I USED TO RESPOND: I WANT TO BE LIKE MONSIEUR DIOR…”

Jean-Paul

GAULTIER

TO ATTEND ONE OF JEAN-PAUL GAULTIER'S SHOWS MEANS BEING HURLED INTO A COLORFUL, EXUBERANT, ENTERTAINING, AND ASTOUNDING WORLD, POPULATED BY DANCERS, SAILORS, PRINCESSES, SIRENS, PIRATES, CHIC GRANNIES, EVEN A TRACKING SHOT OF AMY WINEHOUSE—PUT ON SHOW NOT LONG AFTER THE BRITISH POP ICON'S TRAGIC DEATH.

The *enfant terrible* of French fashion, as he loved to call himself in his youth, regales the public with true and proper spectacles, rather than mere fashion shows. Events rich in provocation and amazing stunts.

Born in 1952, Jean-Paul Gaultier spent his childhood in Arcueil, barely two kilometers south of Paris. His life revolved around his beloved, and eccentric grandmother with her uncontrollable passion for clothes, and her gifts as a fortune-teller. Jean-Paul watched her sewing weird outfits, and stuffed his toy animals with the leftover material. He was fascinated by her little vials of perfume, by the corsets she kept in a trunk. He made bracelets for her by cutting up old tin cans.

The young Gaultier did not study fashion, but what he wanted to do, when he grew up, was always clear to him. At 18, after sending his sketches to all of the most important Parisian houses without receiving any response, he decided to go knocking on the door of Pierre Cardin. The master received him, and, struck by his eccentric appearance—platinum blonde hair, kilt, and striped *Breton* shirt that was, later, to become his personal trademark—decided to give him a try. Gaultier was very talented but also very restless. Not a year had passed before he left Cardin to test his fortune with tailor Jacques Esterel, and afterwards with the House of Patou. Italian in origin and a wise and generous mentor, Pierre Cardin welcomed his pupil back, in 1974, assigning him to several collections meant for the American market. Two years later Gaultier was ready to strike out on his own. In 1976 he established his dressmaker's shop

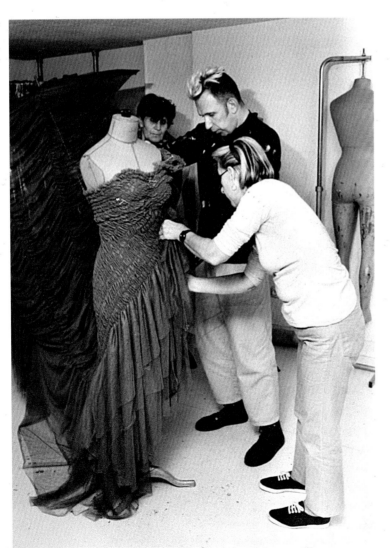

His debut show was the talk of the fashion world. Confronted by transparent tutus, emerging from beneath fishermen's sweaters, as well men in kilts, the international press proclaimed the birth of a new and irreverent talent in Parisian fashion. From that moment, the stylistic trademarks of his products were to be provocation and amusement.

Jean-Paul Gaultier broke down the barriers between masculine and feminine, between over and under, and mixed his and her wardrobes, designing skirt-pants for women and pants-skirts for men, while placing lingerie over outer garments. His runway was "democratic." Over the years he hosted the beautiful and the ugly, the thin and the fat, the young and the old, subverting the unwritten rules of the fashion world. A Greek model with a prominent nose; an old woman in revealing clothes; Beth Ditto, the extra-large front woman of indie rock band *Gossip*; a couple bound by one garment, which began with her, wrapped around him, and then unrolled like a bandage—part of the 1985 Spring/Summer collections with the telling title "A wardrobe for two."

212 Jean-Paul Gaultier at work with seamstresses in his Paris atelier: the production of an evening gown requires meticulous attention to every detail.

213 A portrait of Gaultier appeared in Spanish Vogue in November 2006. The designer's "uniform" and iconic fashion item, the sailor shirt, has been transformed into a fabulous garment with a kilt covered in fluffy feathers.

MOST FAMOUS AMONG HIS NUMEROUS, AND AMAZING, SARTORIAL INVENTIONS, IS THE BODICE WITH TOPSTITCHED CONICAL CUPS, IMMORTALIZED BY MADONNA. IN 1990, THE STAR TURNED TO GAULTIER FOR HER 1990 BLOND AMBITION TOUR. HE CREATED SATIN CORSELETS WITH RIBBED WAIST-LINES, AND THE UNFORGETTABLE ARMORED BRA THAT ENTERED THE COLLECTIVE IMAGINATION.

In the meantime, came the children's line (1988) and casual dress—Gaultier jeans (1992). Gaultier devoted himself to design, to costumes for theater, ballet, and the art films of Peter Greenaway and Pedro Almovódar. His first perfume enshrined his popularity—in the shape of a bust, fastened in a corset, and enclosed in a tin can.

"The way in which I combine motifs and fabrics may be disconcerting," he admitted in an interview with *Vogue*, in 1984, "but what I'm trying to do is provoke new ideas about how clothing items can be brought together in different ways. I think this is a more modern way of wearing clothes that in themselves are rather classic."

Gaultier is still enlivening fashion week in Paris—perhaps no longer as disconcertingly, but certainly still flamboyant, colorful and entertaining, an ode to a life in which opposites attract, cultures mix, and genres are superimposed. A fashion that unites and overthrows clichés.

214 left A sketch, from the *enfant terrible* of French fashion, made for Madonna's Blond Ambition World Tour in 1990. It was the star herself who turned to him to create her stage costumes, some of which were auctioned at Christie's in 2012.

214 right Gaultier's invention becomes a cult object: the silk corset with conical cups, worn by Madonna during her 1990 world tour, entered pop culture history, immortalizing its designer.

215 The armored corset theme in the 2012 Fall/ Winter collection. The evolution of the iconic cape called for an elaborate mesh of metallic strips to create a cage effect.

216 and 217 In his 2003-2004 Fall/Winter collection, Jean-Paul Gaultier was inspired by the concept of high-tech metamorphosis. Gaultier's runway models resembled robot soldiers adorned with surreal details and accessories.

218 An item in the 2012 Fall/Winter collection inspired by the French writer George Sand, who scandalized Paris, in the mid 19th-century, by wearing tuxedos and men's clothing. All of Gaultier's shows are a declaration of love for Paris.

219 An irrepressible parody of "Dancing with the Stars," with lots of competing couples and judges, the 2014 Spring/Summer collection is a genuine Gaultier spectacle. Models and celebrities on the runway. Here Karlie Kloss poses before actress Rossy de Palma, the muse of Almodóvar, and other members of the jury.

220 A sample from Gaultier's 2011 Spring/Summer collection. "Anarchy in the UK," "London Calling," "Vicious," "I Am an Anarchist," are the names given by him to outfits in his collection, reinterpretations of the London punk movement à la couture mode.

221 Another highlight of the 2014 Spring/Summer collection. A dress with a slit, and a bull's eye on its side, reveals the tattoo of a model transformed into a clone of Amy Winehouse for the occasion.

Martin

MARGIELA

MARTIN MARGIELA IS THE STYLIST WHO DOES NOT EXIST.

Enter his name into any search engine and the results may surprise you. The almost total lack of images of his face is remarkable. In an era of star-designers, when visibility, and even overexposure, seems to mean so much, Margiela stands out by virtue of his discretion and seeming aversion to publicity. Only three facial images attest to the actual flesh-and-blood existence of one of the few designers of the last quarter of the 20th-century capable of commanding a respect so intense that it borders on pious veneration among his legions of loyal admirers.

The earliest image dates back to 1983, a second—apparently "stolen"—is from 1997 and a third, undated, depicts him wearing an Iggy Pop t-shirt, an image which we also find in his 1990 collection. The number of interviews he has given over the course of his 20-year career can be counted on the fingers of one hand. Public appearances, to welcome applause at the conclusion of fashion shows, simply don't happen. It's as simple as that.

Since his arrival on the scene, the designer, born in Genk, Belgium, in 1957, a 1979 graduate of the Royal Academy of Fine Arts in Antwerp—just before the famous "Antwerp Six," with whom he is often mistakenly associated—has taken a radical and, paradoxically, revolutionary, position: that of speaking exclusively through his creations. Avoiding high society and public appearances at all costs, he expresses his message only through his work. Conceptual and complex, it is invariably loaded with other layers of meaning, and yet, unlike many others, remains so "universal" as to be capable of dressing any type of physique.

In 1984, Margiela began working in Paris alongside Jean-Paul Gaultier, the *enfant terrible* of French fashion. Later, in 1988, he, along with the Belgian vendor, Jenny Meirens, founded his label, which made its debut with a 1989 Spring/Summer collection. Margiela's extremist and, in his own way, provocative, approach could only shock the fashion establishment. In his work, the idea of contemporary elegance undergoes a comprehensive and head-on review, from which emerges—after a dispute as violent as it is intelligent—a revitalized concept of luxury itself, renewed and regenerated by the designer.

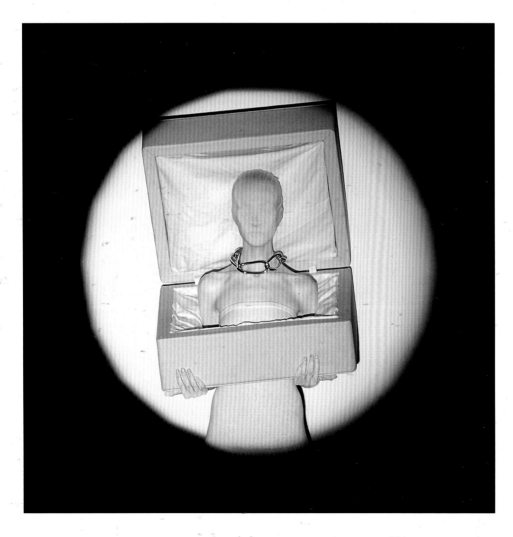

In contrast, Margiela does not present himself as an "individual," but as a collective. People do not speak about Martin, but about the "House of Martin Margiela." The creation of fashion is a team effort, but few are willing to admit it and to share responsibility and honor with their creative team. Margiela definitely goes against the grain and does so, and to the extent that his label, acquired in 2002 by the Italian OTB group ('Only The Brave') led by Renzo Rosso, has survived the designer's sudden departure, in 2009, with undiminished success and without substantial upheavals.

224 White, the signature color of the House, dominates the original human installation on which the jewels of collection number 12 are going to be exhibited.

225 The outfit with a maxi collar, in the 2008-2009 Fall/Winter collection, a classic of the label, which plays with micro and macro proportions.

His aesthetic is based on a truly profound knowledge of traditional haute couture techniques which even earned him the position of artistic director of that most luxurious and bourgeois of labels, Hermès, between 1997 and 2003, a business which he has analyzed, investigated, stripped down and rebuilt on the basis of some completely novel strategies. "Deconstruction" is the magic word and the keystone of his style. Everything that existed before the age of Margiela, he has disassembled, piece by piece, and reassembled in a surprising, unexpected and, at times, illogical new order. Seams showing. Visibly cut edges. Sloppy finishes. Exposed, rather than concealed, hems. Straps sewn on the outside of jackets. The tiniest of details are magnified without restriction while bulkier ones are minimized. The ambiguity between micro and macro is a common thread. Yet, despite all this, novelty is never an end in itself, nor pursued at any cost. On the contrary. Among the most ingenious of Margiela's ideas is *Replica*, a capsule collection that, each season, issues rejuvenated clothing items and accessories unearthed from vintage markets by the designer's team.

Even if achieved unintentionally, however, originality is one of the most distinctive features of the Margiela stylistic trajectory. In 1990, his Tabi boots, inspired by Japanese Tabi socks that resemble certain types of cloven animal hooves, made history, as did his topless sandals: a simple sole attached to the foot with adhesive tape.

Among the milestones of his intense history is the flat collection, with its rigid, two-dimensional items, easily stored in drawers, or the 1996 photoprint collection with its "photocopies" of a broad variety of fabrics printed on silk crepe giving a *trompe l'oeil* effect—a marvelous approach that takes to heart lessons from Belgian surrealist René Magritte. When it comes to choosing materials, Margiela's imagination, similarly, brooks no limit or restraint, but, instead, indulges in its natural inclination to recycle: vinyl LPs, plastic, burlap, combs, or playing cards. Almost anything can be recycled and enter the House's Artisinal collection.

Items, and the way they are presented, are original. Every runway show is a happening, an event, a theatrical coup. Unusual locations, models with hooded faces, "on wheels," replaced by hangers or even a human sandwich on the catwalk, with photos of the collection's items instead of the items themselves.

Similarly original is the image of the brand, every inch of which is recognizable and identifiable by the absolute neutrality of the color white. The label's outlets are white throughout. The staff wear white shirts. Purchases are given to customers in white shopping bags, and each item has an external white label, affixed by four white stitches, which show the numbers 0 to 23, one of which is circled to indicate to which collection the item belongs. With this kind of secret code, intended to replace the terribly overused "logo" that made the fortunes of the most desirable labels of the 1980s and 1990s, he has invented a new, seemingly neutral but actually more powerful, iconic and evocative "logo" than any of the others.

227 A *trompe l'oeil* creates the impression of a double-breast, printed in relief, on the dress worn by the model, whose face has been "erased" to focus attention on the designer's creation.

228 A bride on the 2009-2010 Fall/Winter collection runway. A "nuptial" veil with large white polka dots stands out from the completely nude look.

229 Nude body color, almost eliminating the idea of clothing. In the 2009 Spring/Summer collection, even the face of the model seems to have been "erased" and stripped of any defining features. The red shoulder bag, and traces of the macro shoulder straps, are all that remain.

230 and 231 Two samples from the 2011 Spring/Summer collection, drawn by the House of Martin Margiela collective after the departure of the label's founder. The blouse, transformed and conceptualized, has been squared off into something of a caricature.

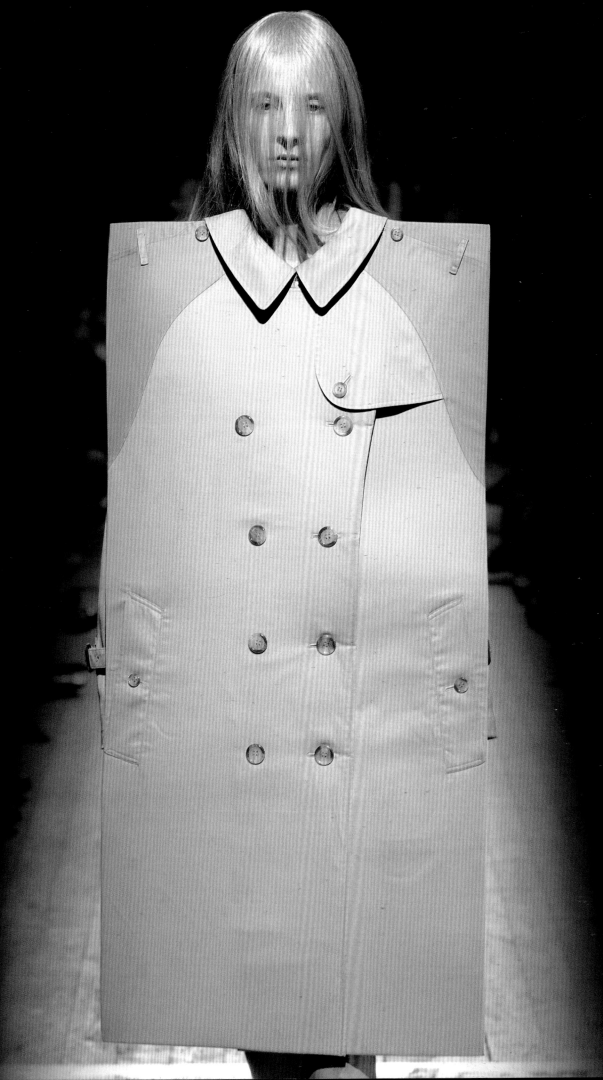

DOLCE & GABBANA

"THE TALENT OF A DESIGNER LIES IN THE ACT OF DESIGNING DRESSES THAT WILL BE UNDERSTOOD

THERE ARE NOT MANY POWER COUPLES IN THE WORLD OF FASHION.

When they do exist, they usually consist of a hand and a brain, a creative type and a strategist, an "absolutely crazy genius" and an alter-ego, who operates, ponders, and reasons in the background. In short, of a creative prodigy and a business-oriented, entrepreneur.

This is not the case with Domenico Dolce and Stefano Gabbana, who have been a fixture on the runway for almost thirty years, and who have always divided and shared the responsibilities, and honors, of what is, probably, the ultimate, grandest brand that Italian fashion has ever produced and thrust onto the international luxury stage.

They evoke a love of Italy and all things Italian, the *Bel Paese*, its tradition, and even the most hackneyed, and taken for granted, aspects of it. Yet their seductive power is so compelling. The art, landscapes, craftsmanship and even cuisine of 'the Boot' (Italy) spill out from their collections, baroque, and over-the-top, triumphs of sensual, fleshy, natural, and irrepressible femininity—the qualities of so much vintage Italian cinema, from Sophia Loren to Lucia Bosè, from Anna Magnani to Silvana Mangano, screen icons who, as the two designers themselves often admit, inspire them.

If the Italy of *La Dolce Vita* (1960) is the designers' inexhaustible source of inspiration, then sunny Sicily, with its beauty—sometimes violent, sometimes fragile, and sophisticated—is their favorite Eden. For Dolce, born in Polizzi Generosa, Sicily, in 1958, this was practically inevitable. For Gabbana, born in Milan four years later, it was a conscious and passion-driven choice.

The two met in the early 1980s, in Milan, the epicenter of an exciting and sparkling collision of the sartorial fashion world and the world of dynamic industrial design that made way for the golden age of "Made in Italy."

234 The two designers gazing at their muse: the model and actress Monica Bellucci, a symbol of Italian femininity and the label's icon.

235 The models on the 2006 Spring/Summer collection runway have ears of wheat in their hands and hair, as if coming out of a barn. On the label's 20th anniversary, Dolce & Gabbana celebrate the provocative and sensual beauty of Italy. Tight corsets and romantic lace, seemingly pulled out of grandma's trunk, are the collection's leitmotifs.

THEIR RUNWAY DEBUT CAME IN OCTOBER 1985 DURING MILAN'S FASHION WEEK, WHEN THEY presented their *Real Women* collection against a homespun—not to say paltry—stage set composed, according to legend, of Dolce's bed sheets. In their very first signature collections there was already clear evidence of the stylistic elements that would characterize their women: well-pronounced curves, sinuous hour-glass silhouettes, dresses with a 'bustier' look, naughty black lace, yet also the use of men's textiles, such as twill and pinstripes, creations from beneath which peeked through mischievous bras. These were the same fabrics that clothed their men when they were not dressed down for comfort.

The Dolce & Gabbana style is instantly recognizable, and is perfectly superimposed over a feminine ideal that is simultaneously feisty and insolent, chaste and erotic. The black "Sicilian dress" with its clinging bustier, shoulder straps, pilfered from the world of lingerie, and a petticoat-like skirt, has become an icon, the leitmotif and trademark of their style, and one that they offer again and again, always the same but always up-dated, season after season.

Madonna was the first and greatest of the stars of pop-music to declare their devotion to the label. So much so that she was proud to have herself photographed washing dishes, like a housewife, in an advertising campaign. She has Italian blood, as does Isabella Rossellini, the muse and incarnation of the purer, more concentrated Dolce & Gabbana style, who, as icon of the brand until the late 1990s, passed the baton to Monica Bellucci, the only true diva of Italian cinema during the last few decades and the star of a legendary commercial, directed by Oscar winning Giuseppe Tornatore, for one of the many Dolce & Gabbana perfumes.

In just a few years, the "Gilbert & George" of Italian fashion, as the two have been described—perhaps with a little perspicacity—succeeded in building an empire that reached to the stars. Aside from adding a second, irreverent junior line, Dolce & Gabbana expanded its market with top-selling perfumes, and underwear collections, which made the name visible above the waists of the low-cut jeans worn by the world's teenagers. Their popularity has been constantly rising. Perhaps the best scene from the movie *The Devil Wears Prada* (2006) is the one in which the intern, Andrea, answering a phone call meant for the executive director of the prestigious fashion magazine, *Runway*, naïvely asks: "Can you please spell 'Gabbana'?" and the caller hangs up.

They churn out their women's fashion collections fearlessly, one after another, with the most stereotypical fallacies about their chosen island, each time succeeding in re-dressing them with a patina of glamor in which irony, inevitably, plays its part: from puppets to carriages, from Caltagirone porcelain to the mosaics of Piazza Armerina, from marzipan to Indian figs, from eggplants to Agrigento's Valley of the Temples. Their models, often youngsters recruited from the street, strut across the runway to the notes of the purest Italian melodies, sung perhaps by Luciano Pavarotti or Domenico Modugno. But it is the more recent voice of the Black Eyed Peas that continues the popular myth to a hip-hop rhythm: *"I drive these brothers crazy / I do it on the daily / They treat me really nicely / They buy me all these ices / Dolce & Gabbana..."*

238 An item inspired by Elsa Schiaparelli in the 2009-2010 Fall/Winter collection. The face of Marilyn Monroe projects from the voluminous skirt of the evening gown.

239 The 2008-2009 Fall/Winter collection concludes with the usual panoply of crinolines and full skirts, one aspect of the designers' classic repertoire.

240 Gold coins, with profiles borrowed from Magna Grecia, cover the bodice of a dress in the 2014 Spring/Summer collection. The Temple of Segesta, Agrigento's Valley of the Temples—Sicily is the chief source of inspiration for the two designers.

241 Like Vestal Virgins of style, covered with the costliest gilt embroidery, models make their final exit from the 2014 Spring/Summer collection.

242 Inspired by pottery from Caltagirone, an ornate wedge from the 2014 Spring/Summer collection. Domenico Dolce and Stefano Gabbana love to reminisce about all the many facets of 'their' Sicily.

243 Sicilian dolls reproduced on a blouse in the 2013 Spring/Summer collection. The island's folklore and tradition dominated the runway.

244 The Byzantine mosaics of the Cathedral of Monreale are the point of departure for the 2013-2014 Fall/Winter collection.

245 Chastity and
sensuality, transparency
and religious symbolism;
the recurring black
lace in the designer's
products, on the one
hand, and the crowned
head of St. Agatha,
patron saint of Catania,
on the other.

"MY ROLE IS THAT OF SEDUCING."

John
GALLIANO

"MY ROLE IS THAT OF SEDUCING."

IF WE COULD SEARCH THROUGH JOHN GALLIANO'S BOX OF MEMORIES, WE WOULD CERTAINLY FIND A FADED PHOTOGRAPH FROM 1984 DEPICTING CAPTIVATING REVOLUTIONARIES WITH HIGH BOOTS AND DECONSTRUCTED FROCK-COATS, INSPIRED BY THE DANDIES OF THE FRENCH REVOLUTION.

Les Incroyables was the collection he prepared for his diploma, at Central Saint Martins College of Art and Design, which ended up in the windows of the prestigious London boutique, Browns. We would also find memories of a very young Kate Moss in crinoline. We would also discover memories of Diana Princess of Wales at a gala in New York, wearing a blue petticoat lined with black lace, memories of all of yesterday's and today's top models covered in multi-colored garments, inspired by the paintings of Cocteau and Picasso, Monet and Boldini, Raphael, Tiepolo, Michelangelo, and Leonardo, and finally, Charlize Theron in a violet bustier dress, at the Oscars. In addition, we would find memories of his investiture with a CBE, by the Queen, for his achievements in the world of fashion and with the Legion d'Honneur, by President Sarkozy of France.

From this overstuffed album, however, would slip several newspaper cuttings. Who knows if Galliano had deliberately saved them, certainly he had not forgotten them, the bearers of bad news and portents of future woes. "Galliano accused of anti-Semitism," "Dior sues Galliano." Such were the worldwide headlines between March and September of 2011, as the designer was hit by scandal for having hurled racist insults at a couple in a Paris bar. He received a 6000 Euro fine and was fired from his job.

Ousted from his position as creative director of both Maison Dior and from his own label—both under the control of French multinational LVMH (Louis Vuitton Moët Hennessy)—Galliano was finally forced to make amends, and confront his alcoholism and reliance on sleeping pills. An unpleasant incident, which cost the fashion pirate dearly and cast a shadow on Galliano the man, but which could not obscure the merits of the imaginative, theatrical and flamboyant designer. One could say that the world of Galliano on the runway was a world that unified rather than divided. A world that fed on cultures from all over the world in a musical box of diverse ethnicities and customs. From his very first show, in the auditorium of that fashion school, one of the world's most prestigious, Galliano took the audience into a fantastic and dream-like universe.

248 John Galliano at work in the Grand Salon of the House of Dior on the Avenue Montaigne in Paris.

249 A portrait of the designer, in 2001, as he attentively follows the fitting of one of his creations.

Born in Gibraltar in 1960, John Galliano moved to London with his family at the age of 6. The transition from that colorful and boisterous world, situated on a peninsula between Spain and Morocco—redolent with incense and spices, dotted with multi-colored fabrics and filled with the shouts of vendors—to the grey skies of London, was traumatic. Galliano never forgot that change in color, clothing and culture, and, "the idea of the meeting of cultures"—as he termed it in *Vogue* in 2009—continued to influence his creative experiments.

On the runway, either at Dior, where he was creative director between 1997 and 2011, or his own eponymous label (founded in 1993), he introduced reminiscences of distant lands, real and imaginary, exotic insinuations, cinematic mementos, dream-like voyages and sophisticated fables, in spectacular shows animated by his taste for theatricality and amazing scenography.

At Dior, he riffled through the archives to revive the dream. Cosmopolitan ladies, mademoiselles who seemed to materialize from the sketches of René Gruau, the House's historical illustrator. Women inspired by Madame Bricard, known as Mitzah, Christian Dior's muse, and by Maria Lani, in portraits by Matisse and Chagall. He paid tribute to Christian Dior's favorite artists, and on the occasion of the House's sixtieth anniversary, put on the *Ball of the Artists*, an unforgettable fashion event.

In love with the history of costume, Galliano drew inspiration from Spanish, Japanese and French culture. In a game of cross references and citations, he brought to life the geishas of Puccini's memory, empresses, flamenco dancers, half-dressed *merveilleuses* from the early 1900s, modern Joans of Arc and elegant Cleopatras, colorful Marie Antoinettes, and a Mother Nature bedecked in flowers.

More recently, after his fall from grace, and exclusion from the world of fashion, he prepared Kate Moss's wedding dress for her marriage to Jamie Hince. For him, the long, romantic, 1920s-inspired gown, in which the supermodel went to the altar, was an opportunity for creative rebirth, which, in the wake of his depression, restored his will to work.

In the July 2013 issue of *Vanity Fair*, John Galliano gave an exclusive interview that hinted at his return. So, when will the next act of the spectacle begin? We cannot say. What we do know is that 29 years of fervent creative activity have already granted him a place atop the Mount Olympus of those designers who have made their mark on the history of fashion.

250 The pirate of fashion, photographed before a portrait of Christian Dior. Galliano was creative director of the House of Dior between 1997 and 2011.

251 Detail of a jacket, with festoons over the shoulders, from a sample in the 2005 Spring/ Summer collection. The fabric, printed with newspaper articles about the designer, was inspired by Elsa Schiaparelli.

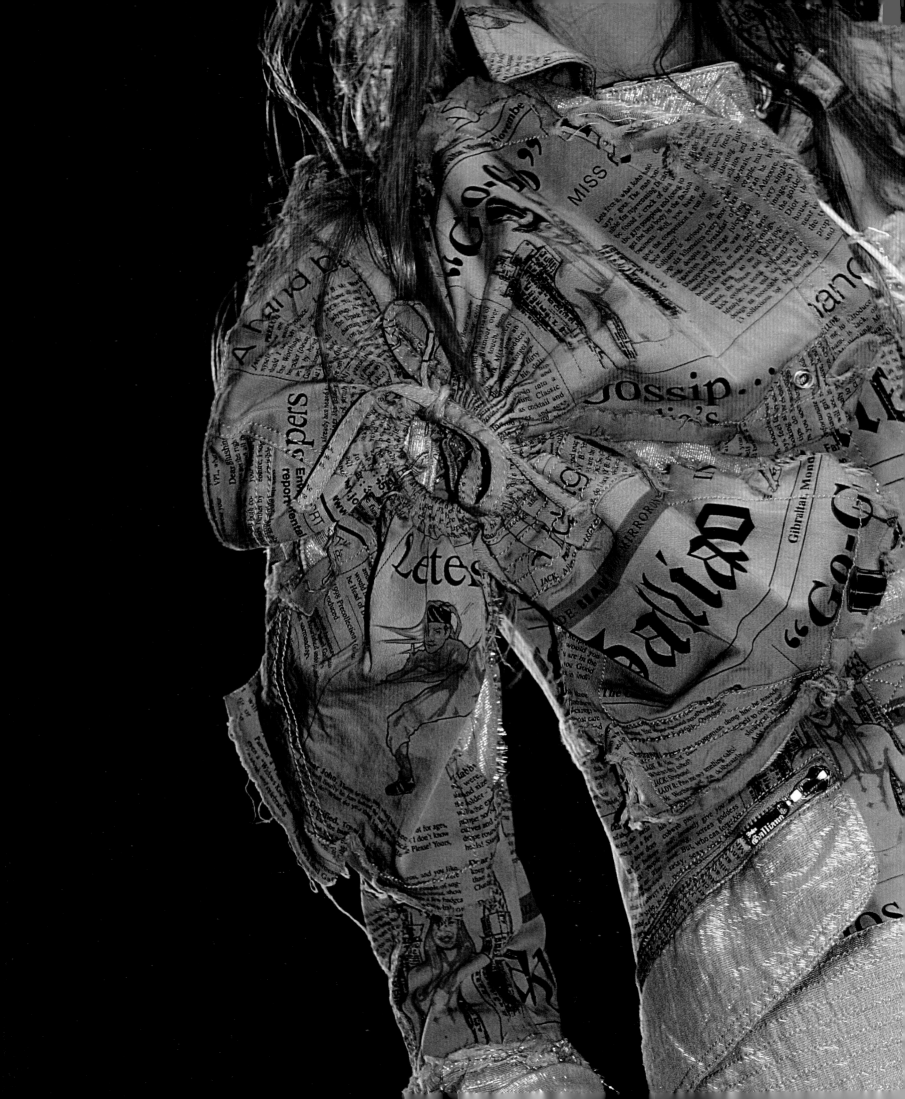

252 A creation by John Galliano, for the Dior 2005-2006 Fall/Winter collection. A journey among fantasy angels that begins and ends with a horse-drawn carriage.

253 John Galliano's 2004-2005 Fall/Winter collection was a colorful and psychedelic spectacle, rich with innuendo. The Yemeni tribe, which Galliano considered his source of inspiration, along with corsets and crinolines, breathed life into majestic outfits in a couture gypsy mode.

John Galliano

254 Inspired by Flemish painters and the Christian Dior archive, Dior's 2009 Spring/Summer collection, designed by Galliano.

255 A detail from a Dior dress with an embroidered border, worn over shoes with sculpted heels.

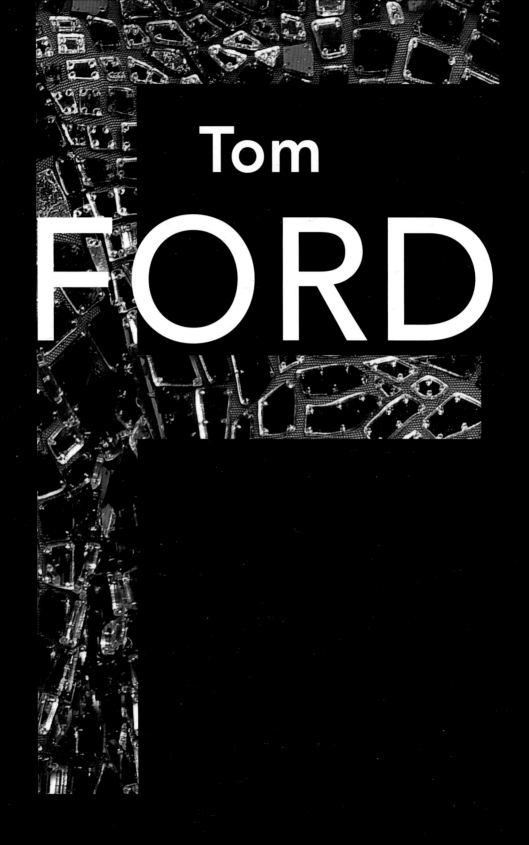

Tom
FORD

"I'M LUCKY, I HAVE MASS-MARKET TASTES.
WHEN I SAY I LIKE A SHOE, GENERALLY THOUSANDS OF PEOPLE WILL LIKE IT

And living proof that artists can be born anywhere is Tom Ford, even in Texas, in the far South of the United States. Far, very far, from the historic poles of fashion. Far from iconic Paris and ingenious Milan, and even from unpredictable New York. Far from everything.

Thomas Carlyle "Tom" Ford, was born in Austin, Texas, in the summer of 1961. When he was little more than a child, his family moved to Santa Fe, New Mexico. But when it was time to decide where to go to college, and particularly to study architecture, Tom had no doubts; the city that never sleeps seemed to be waiting exclusively for him. While in New York he met Andy Warhol, and his entourage, at his legendary hang-outs, starting with Studio 54. It was in these places, and during those legendary years, with their rapid burn-out, that Ford stock-piled, in his memory, suggestions, auras, and undertones, which, like a seemingly inexhaustible font, were to feed his creativity for years to come. A cheeky and audacious beauty, shameless in its opulence, and almost arrogant in the way it played cops-and-robbers with vulgarity, ruled his imagination, which from the very outset, comprised sex, luxury, and power—a trinity that was anything but holy

While still in attendance at Parsons, The New School for Design, Ford spent more than a year in Paris, where he did an internship at the Chloé press office. It was during this time that he realized that fashion was to be his destiny. When he returned to the United States, he succeeded in finding a job in the style department of designer Cathy Hardwick; a mere two years later, he moved on to Perry Ellis, where the creative director was, the little known, Marc Jacobs. At precisely the time that Jacobs was extolling the virtues of the phenomenon known as 'grunge,' which was to leave its mark on the 1990s, Ford was embarked on a trajectory—radically opposed to grunge—that would make his fortune.

In 1990, Gucci took him on to its creative team. With its fame somewhat diminished, the Florentine house was certainly not at the peak of its splendor. A perfect testing ground for going all-out, for patenting that enterprising and cheeky "formula Ford" that the designer would one day register as his unmistakable signature. Part sensuality, part provocation, part ostentation: shake well and serve chilled. There was no lack of tension with management. Maurizio Gucci "always wanted everything round and brown, and Tom wanted it square and black."

The facts, and sales figures, proved the designer to be right.

260 A portrait of the designer in a minimalist setting that contrasts with his rich, bold, opulent style.

261 The sexy, chic version of the hippie style in a look signed by Gucci and conceived by his Texan designer.

With the help of star photographer Mario Testini, and headstrong stylist Carine Roitfeld, future director of *Vogue Paris*, Ford breathed life and spirit into a brand that was not in the least reassuring, but on the contrary, almost dangerous. One that catalyzed the desires of rich women all over the world not only thanks to its plunging necklines, expensive rhinestone-studded and feather-adorned jeans, and complacently exposed nudity, but also to a marvelously orchestrated poster campaign, geared to provoke interest—of whatever kind—and, thus, enhance its desirability, as in the very first ad, which depicted a young boy kneeling before a woman, who, lowering her briefs, uncovered her pudenda shaved in the shape of a G. Tom Ford, albeit a talented designer, is first and foremost a genius of communication. Few have been as adept as he at creating a global image, a dream, perhaps with a touch of perversion, and an entire universe to covet from afar, or in which to be immersed to the neck. Ford is essentially a marketing man on loan to fashion.

In a certain sense, he himself is marketed as a product: handsome, sun-tanned, alluring, sexy, he personally volunteers himself as a testimonial to his own aesthetic.

In 2000, he was also appointed as creative director of Yves Saint Laurent, a label that had just been acquired by the Gucci group. Here, too, he did not scrimp with provocation. The campaign launching its men's fragrance M7 used a totally naked model. And never mind if it was Yves Saint Laurent in person who declared "The poor man does what he can," because success had always been on the side of the Texan who had thrown Paris off balance.

The love affair with Gucci ended in March 2004; Ford's last show for the label marked the end of an era, that of extremism at all cost, to make room for the restraint that the crisis, perhaps still on the distant horizon, seemed to portend.

Ford knew how to distance himself from the scene, silently, making himself the subject of discussion more by his absence than by his presence. He also demonstrated his enviable competence by generating a restless waiting period for his comeback. In 2005, along with his partner Dominico De Sole, he founded his own label. But although everybody was expecting a grand debut with a collection of women's apparel, the designer, again, surprised his followers. The new "dream," underwritten by Tom Ford, began with diva sunglasses and a series of deluxe perfumes that immediately entered the collective imagination. The next stage saw him as the leading light in the creation of a collection of men's apparel, freely "inspired" by more formal canons of elegance dating back to the 1950s. Canons splendidly personified in Professor George, the lead character in *A Single Man* (2009), magnificently portrayed by Colin Firth, in Ford's acclaimed directorial debut.

It was only in September 2010, after opening imposing flagship stores in a string of great international luxury-good capitals, from London to New York, that Ford presented his first signature collection of womenswear. Nevertheless, in an era ruled by over-exposure, he again went against the current, with a bullet-proof show, not using models but show business stars, from Julianne Moore to Beyoncé Knowles, to Lauren Hutton; the number of invited journalists was tightly restricted, and there was tight security regarding photos of the event, and its outfits, until the moment when the invited guests entered the stores—a successful and miraculous marriage of luxury and pop. "I'm lucky, I have mass-market tastes. When I say I like a shoe, generally thousands of people will like it." So proclaims King Midas of Texas.

262 Mystery is one of the mainstays of Tom Ford's style, made clear in this outfit from the 2003-2004 Fall/Winter collection. The maxi collar, in an unreleased white version, hides the face of the dark model on the runway.

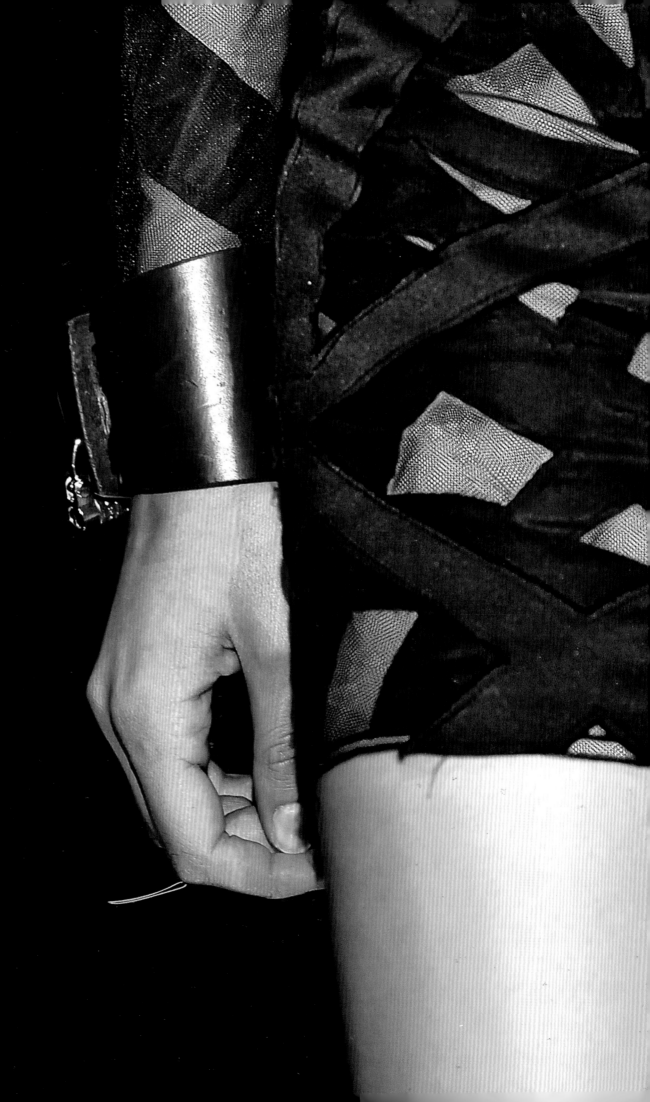

264 Hints of sadomasochism
are evident in the shoes of the
2013 Spring/Summer collection,
embellished with a decidedly
original bejeweled heel.

265 The body, veiled and,
simultaneously, unveiled: the
eternal game of revealing
and concealing are frequently
recurring elements of sensuality
as interpreted by the American
designer. This game can also be
seen on the runway of the 2014
Spring/Summer collection.

266 The savage sensuality of animal prints is reinterpreted by Tom Ford in an uber-chic key, as in this intricately embroidered zebra print, embellished with feathers, in the 2013-2014 Fall/Winter collection.

267 Sophisticated embroidery on a spectacular see-through dress in the 2013-2014 Fall/Winter collection, presented on the runway during London Fashion Week.

268 High-necked, but deeply sensual, the crystal-bedecked dress worn by an Asian model on the runway of the 2014 Spring/Summer collection.

269 A detail from an exquisite dress in the 2014 Spring/Summer collection reveals the myriad colors of the tiny geometric mirrors from which it is made—a modern mosaic with a disco effect that exudes femininity and sex appeal.

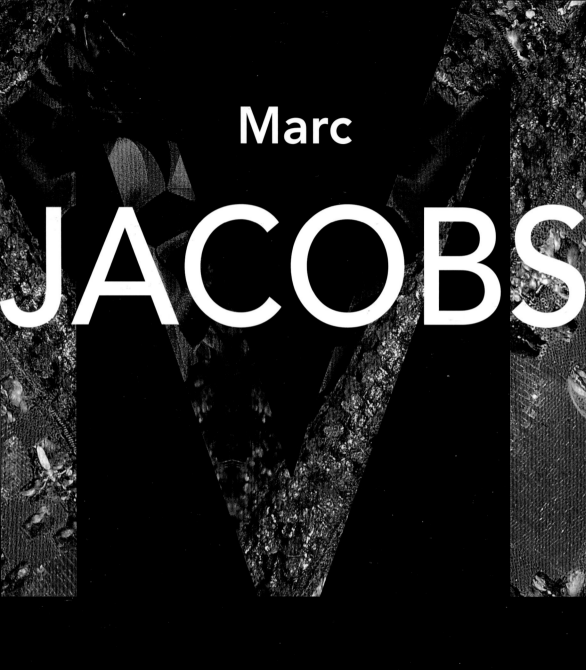

Marc
JACOBS

"IT'S THE THINGS THAT AREN'T ACCEPTED AS CONVENTIONALLY BEAUTIFUL
THAT I FIND MORE ATTRACTIVE."

NAKED, WITH A LOUIS VUITTON SPEEDY BAG OR AN ENORMOUS BOTTLE OF PERFUME COVERING GENITALIA. VACUUMING, IN AN EMBROIDERED GREEN ORGANZA GOWN, IN A VIDEO THAT INSTANTLY WENT VIRAL. STALKED BY PAPARAZZI, AS IF HE WERE A CELEBRITY ON THE BEACHES OF RIO, WHILE PASSIONATELY KISSING HIS 24-YEAR-OLD PORN-STAR FIANCÉ. IN PAJAMAS, WEARING A KILT, IN A WOMAN'S FUCHSIA GOWN, DRESSED IN TRANSPARENT LACE AND WHITE BOXERS, AT A MET GALA IN NEW YORK.

We are accustomed to seeing him this way, but before he became the good-looking hunk of today, Marc Jacobs was a neurotic New Yorker of the sort we expect to see more in a Woody Allen movie than backstage at a fashion show, wearing spectacles, worn sneakers, and a cigarette dangling from his mouth. In his nerd or macho version, he is, in any event, always, and in each instance, provocative, ironic, and ingenious.

The best known and most unpredictable of American designers, and the youngest ever to be awarded the Council of Fashion Designers of America (CFDA) award, the fashion Oscar, in the New Fashion Talents category, Marc Jacobs comes up with something new and unexpected with every collection. Combining elements inspired by couture and street-culture, the cosmopolitan ethnicity and aesthetics of the Big Apple, old and new, the fashion of the past and contemporary zeitgeist, he brings onstage a harmonic and well-calibrated mix of heterogeneous charms and features.

His fashion events are the most eagerly anticipated in New York's fashion week, provocations that break with all modes, which delight and dazzle the world of fashion twice a year while delineating future trends.

Marc Jacobs was born in New York on April 9, 1963. In 1984 he designed a collection of over-sized polka-dotted sweaters that won him numerous awards at Parsons The New School for Design and that ended up in the windows of Charivari, a trend-setting avant-garde boutique in Manhattan.

His first shows won over the press. But the one that placed his name on the list of the most promising designers of the era was that of November 1992. Representing Perry Ellis, a sports clothing label, of which he was artistic director, Jacobs exhibited a deliberately scruffy layered look, with flannel shirts and combat boots inspired by the grunge movement. Introducing the pop culture of Nirvana and MTV to the runway cost him his job, but earned him the enthusiasm of the public and the press. Despite being fired by Perry Ellis, Marc Jacobs acquired the reputation of a prophet, of one able to predict future fashion.

272 The unmistakable monogram 'LV' liberally covers the hat, jacket, and top of the brand model of Louis Vuitton, the prestigious House specializing in luxury leather goods, of which Jacobs was creative director between 1997 and 2013.

273 The Influence and inspiration of various eras of modern fashion come together in Jacob's work, reinterpreted through a distorted lens that loves to flirt with kitsch, as shown in the 2009-2010 Fall/ Winter collection, where a super-feminine bustier was offset by a pair of gentleman's slacks.

In 1993 he founded the Marc Jacobs International Company, with his partner Robert Duffy. His fashion, so intensely contemporary that it draws liberally from the street, and was defined by Jacobs as "a little preppy, a little grungy, a little couture," won over girls with strong personalities who like to express their 'look' with designer labels and a mix of pieces bought at street markets. His ironic accessories, like the Mouse—ballerina flats with mouse faces, marked with the label 'Marc by Marc Jacobs' (a second line was founded in 2000) are cult items for fashionistas.

In 1997, the French multinational LVMH (Louis Vuitton Moët Hennessy), invited him to revitalize Maison Vuitton. The prêt-à-porter line of the historic, century-old, French label came into being under Marc Jacobs' guidance. Jacobs performed a miracle. In ten years sales quadrupled. He reinvented the Speedy, Louis Vuitton's emblematic travel case, and the brand's other iconic bags.

The monogram spread to jeans, to transparent pvc, was transformed into graffiti in the works of the artist and fashion designer Stephen Sprouse, and in watercolors by Richard Prince. Vuitton symbols took the form of cheerful cherry blossoms with colorful eyes, little flowers in the kawaii manner of Japanese artist Takashi Murakami. With Yayoi Kusama, they went on to become multi-colored polka dots of various sizes and densities, and spread to infinity on everything from bags to dresses, scarves, sunglasses and keychains, in the *Dots Infinity* collection.

274 Drawn to past eras in fashion history, which he reinterprets in his own style, Marc Jacobs looked to the silhouette of the 1940s for his 2011-2012 Fall/Winter/ collection. Polka dots are the recurrent and easily recognizable leitmotif of the entire collection.

275 A similar and complimentary world on the Louis Vuitton runway that same season. A subtle sadomasochistic aura in the background is underscored by the brilliance of white collars and the sensuality of black and patent leather details.

276 A feather bodysuit and concierge cap for the model on the runway of the Louis Vuitton 2011-2012 Fall/Winter collection, set in the hall of a former luxury hotel, from whose elevators emerged voluptuous models.

277 Patent leather details in an immaculate white dress, made sexier by a wide belt with a cage effect, in the Louis Vuitton 2011-2012 Fall/Winter collection.

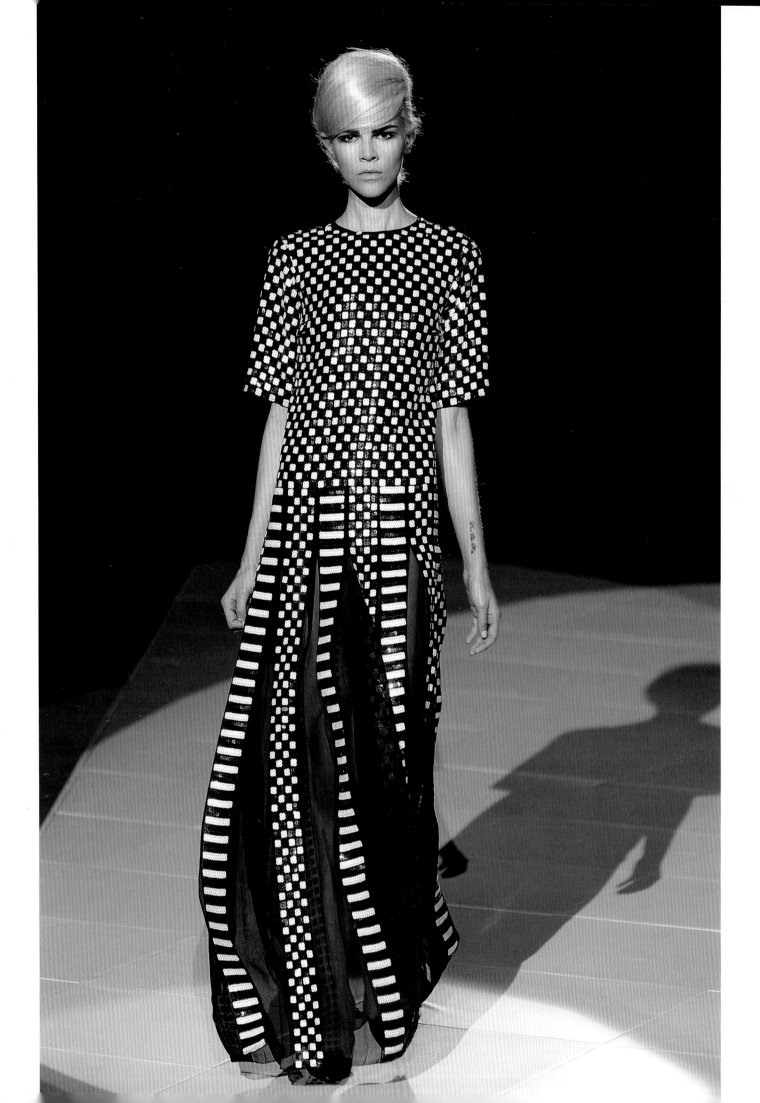

Jacobs rejuvenates the link between fashion and art, which he adores and collects, year after year through exceptional collaborations, mostly with artists, but also with movie directors, like his friend and muse Sofia Coppola, who has designed super-chic reinterpretations of the Speedy and Keepall bags, and Wes Anderson, for whom Jacobs created a set of suitcases and trunks, as well as some of the stage costumes, for *The Darjeeling Limited* (2007).

When, after 16 years of honorable service, Marc Jacobs left Louis Vuitton in October 2013, the House was one of the most desirable and most coveted on the planet. His final show, his 2014 Spring/Summer collection, was a triumph in black that paid tribute to the years he spent at Louis Vuitton and to all the women who had inspired him: from Catherine Deneuve to Lady Gaga, from Kate Moss to Miuccia Prada and Anna Wintour, to name but a few. Henceforth, Marc Jacobs will devote himself entirely to his own brand. And he will continue, no doubt, to leave mouths agape with his fashion and ironic provocations.

278 Marc Jacobs' 2013 Spring/Summer collection was inspired by Optical Art, with its black and white geometric patterns and graphic elements, as well as by Edie Sedgwick and the Factory, from the 1970s.

279 A profusion of black polka dots, of various sizes, adorns clothing and accessories in the 2011-2012 Fall/Winter collection.

Alexander McQUEEN

"THERE'S NO ROAD BACK FOR ME NOW."
"I SHALL TAKE YOU WITH ME ON VOYAGES THAT YOU WOULD NEVER HAVE DEEMED POSSIBLE."

IT WAS OCTOBER 6, 2009, WHEN THE MOST REVOLUTIONARY FASHION SHOW, EVER, WAS STAGED IN PARIS, UNDER THE DIRECTION OF PHOTOGRAPHER AND FILM-MAKER NICK KNIGHT: A FASHION EVENT THAT BROUGHT TO THE RUNWAY A VIDEO OF UNDERWATER MUTANT WOMEN, PROJECTED IN MULTIPLES ONTO A MAXI-SCREEN, TO THE SOUND OF LADY GAGA'S *BAD ROMANCE*, AND WHICH, MORE IMPORTANTLY, WAS TRANSMITTED DIRECTLY ONLINE AND, THUS, ACCESSIBLE TO THE WORLD.

"Every year, buyers and journalists come to attend the spectacle of my fashion shows," so observed McQueen, about his 2010 Spring/Summer collection, in an interview to Women's Wear Daily magazine (WWD). "But I wish to create something different, something for a larger public—for the people in Australia, Asia, and Central America who don't have a seat at the fashion event. What inspires me is world domination! This is the beginning of a new era."

In reality, he was foreseeing the end of a brief but incredibly intense career. The designer took his own life on February 11, 2010, in an extreme act following a deep depression.

Between dream and reality, the most refined sartorial mastery and fantasy, Victorian reminiscence and futuristic cyborg style, romanticism and transgression, light and dark, the visionary genius of McQueen knew how to capture the hearts of all those who love fashion and art. Yes, art, because in certain senses fashion can rightfully be called art—when it challenges fallacies, subverts traditional canons, and places itself at the service of fantasy. And it was in a museum that the nineteen-year career of this "hooligan of fashion," as McQueen was nicknamed for his subversive vein, was exhibited.

On May 4, 2011, the day of the public opening of *Alexander McQueen: Savage Beauty*, the Metropolitan Museum of New York achieved record attendance. Visitors waited in line, anxious to discover something more about the artist, but also about the man who had struggled with depression only to surrender to it and put an end to his life at the age of only forty.

Born in the East End of London, in 1969, Lee Alexander McQueen began to train, as a seventeen-year-old, with tailors Anderson and Sheppard of Savile Row, and afterwards, with theatrical costumiers Bermans & Nathans. During those years, young McQueen picked up the most elaborate dressmaking techniques and became familiar with theater and period costumes, particularly seventeenth century Shakespearean designs.

283 Seen as the last of fashion's great visionaries, McQueen was the maker of astounding, theatrical creations, such as this outfit, covered with feathers and topped off with a headpiece by Philip Treacy, in the 2009-2010 Fall/Winter collection.

282 McQueen in a London portrait from June 1999.

AFTER MOVING CLOSER TO THE WORLD OF PRÊT-À-PORTER FASHION,
WITH THE JAPANESE DESIGNER KOJI TATSUNO, AND AFTERWARDS WORKING IN THE STYLE
DEPARTMENT OF ROMEO GIGLI IN MILAN, HE RETURNED TO LONDON TO COMPLETE HIS STUDIES
AT THE PRESTIGIOUS CENTRAL SAINT MARTINS COLLEGE OF ARTS AND DESIGN.

It was in 1992, at the end of that academic year's fashion show, that his talent was noticed by fashion journalist Isabella Blow, who purchased the entire collection, and from that moment became his mentor and muse. Suzy Menkes, the authoritative spokesperson of the *International Herald Tribune*, was equally struck by that initial collection: "It's rich in exceptional creative material and technical mastery," she wrote; "Plus, the cut and the ornaments are sublime."

The skill of the great couturier, refined on Savile Row, along with the creative flair of the street youth, were forever to remain McQueen's stylistic trademark, even with all the ruckus in the fashion world over his appointment as artistic director at Givenchy, succeeding his fellow countryman, John Galliano, in 1997, and becoming, at not quite thirty years of age, the youngest couturier in history. His collaboration with the French house of fashion lasted until 2001, the year of its acquisition by the Gucci Group, which bought 51% of the Alexander McQueen label. Today, in spite of its founder's death, the label continues on its course under the leadership of his friend, and former right-hand person, Sarah Burton.

Four-time winner of the best UK designer of the year prize, as well as the Council of Fashion Designers of America's (CFDA) International Designer of the Year Award, and invested with the prestigious title of Commander of the Most Excellent Order of the British Empire (CBE) by the Queen for his important contribution to the excellence of English fashion, the *enfant terrible* of fashion was indeed famous for his innovative and experimental collections, but above all for his incredible and theatrical shows.

For everyone, press and buyer, the English designer's runway shows were the most highly anticipated of the season—twenty minutes of pure enchantment, provocative and flamboyant spectacles that never failed to cause a sensation.

284 McQueen's shows were the most keenly anticipated during fashion week—veritable spectacles, unique in their special effects. For his 2003-2004 Fall/Winter collection, he constructed a kind of wind tunnel.

285 The outfits in the 2009-2010 Fall/Winter collection used elements from couture, Dior's New Look, and Chanel's tweed, exaggerating them into parody.

In 1999 he hired model Aimee Mullins, an amputee, to walk down the catwalk on finely carved wooden prostheses. For his 2005 Spring/Summer collection, he staged a human chess game. The next season, he presented his 2006 Fall/Winter collection with a show entitled the *Widows of Culloden*, during which he projected a hologram of Kate Moss on the runway just as England was in uproar over the Kate 'cocaine' scandal. In 2009, in addition to webcasting his fashion show, he presented the Armadillo Shoe, hated by models for its 30 cm. height, but loved by Lady Gaga, who chose to wear them in her video clip *Bad Romance*.

With his gravity-defying, vertiginous heels, sculpted outfits, jewel-encrusted fabrics, metal headpieces, feather coats, impalpable organza and fluttering chiffon, McQueen left not only journalists but the entire jaded fashion industry open-mouthed. In his hands, models became winged goddesses, hybrid beings, semi-cyborgs, semi-mythological creatures who appeared from and disappeared into hidden trapdoors, emerged from glass cubes and reflecting pools, while exhibiting themselves in frenetic twirling dances.

Gifted with inexhaustible creativity, Alexander McQueen was also a creator of "wearable" trends, from unforgettable kimono jackets to *bumsters* pants, with low waist-bands, that left buttocks half-exposed to heighten their erogenous value, to the skull motif, still the trademark of the label's accessories, reproduced on a scarf that became an immediate must-have for fashion addicts around the world.

286 During the 2005-2006 Fall/Winter collection, Lee projected a hologram of Kate Moss onto the runway.

287 On October 6, 2009, McQueen brought female mutants to the catwalk. On their feet, Armadillo Shoes with vertiginous 30-centimeter heels, made famous by Lady Gaga, who chose them for her video *Bad Romance*.

288 A dress entirely covered with white feathers in the 2009-2010 Fall/Winter collection.

289 These dream-like, extraordinary creations, presented in Paris on March 9, 2009, reaffirmed Lee Alexander McQueen as the only contemporary designer driven purely by creativity.

UNIQUE, ASTONISHING, ANTI-ESTABLISHMENT, HIS SARTORIAL CREATIONS HAVE THE POWER TO TRANSPORT US INTO THE REALM OF FANTASY, AND, EVEN MORE, TO TELL US ABOUT THE EMOTIONS OF THEIR CREATOR.

"His fashion was an outlet for his feelings, an expression of the deepest, often dark, facet of his imagination," claimed Andrew Bolton, curator of the retrospective exhibition devoted to the designer, at the Met, in an interview by the English newspaper, *The Guardian*. "He was a true Romantic in the Byronian sense of the word."

Attracted to the sublime more than to beauty, he knew how to bend the laws of aesthetics to the rationale of fantasy, by changing the very meaning of making fashion, and, rightfully, taking part in the shaping of his own history.

The name Lee Alexander McQueen is already a myth.

Dries

VAN NOTEN

"…I AM KNOWN FOR COLOR, PRINTS, AND EMBROIDERIES, AND, USUALLY,
THE MORE THEY CLASH, THE MORE I LIKE THEM."

THERE WERE SIX, AND UNITING THEM WAS THE FACT THAT THEY HAD ALL GRADUATED
FROM ANTWERP'S ROYAL ACADEMY OF FINE ARTS, BETWEEN 1980 AND 1981, AND ARRIVED TOGETHER
ON THE INTERNATIONAL FASHION SCENE IN 1986, IN LONDON.

The *Nouvelle Vague* of avant-garde fashion—experimental, innovative, and anti-establishment—they met with instant and sensational success. As if the world had been waiting for them. A blast of fresh air. A shot of originality.

From a stylistic point of view, the Antwerp Six—as they were immediately labeled, a designation from which each tried to break loose with proud individualistic spirit—had almost nothing in common. Dries Van Noten, Ann Demeulemeester, Dirk Van Saene, Marina Yee, Walter Van Beirendonck, and Dirk Bikkembergs were neither a group, nor a school, but, rather, a wave that fate had allowed to swell. Today, several of them have abandoned the scene. Others have, perhaps, lost their way. Recently, a few have, unexpectedly, said goodbye to fashion altogether. But one has remained, and earned a top position within the panorama of fashion.

Dries Van Noten was born in Antwerp, in 1958. Apparel had run in his family for two generations. His grandfather, a tailor, had mended and refurbished used coats, and garments, during the Second World War. His father had owned two men's clothing stores; his mother had managed yet another one. If not downright inevitable, it was certainly likely that fashion was to enter Dries' life.

His style seemed clear and defined, even in the first menswear collection that he designed, and grew even more so in 1993, when he began devoting himself to women's fashion. A taste for impurity was obvious. The pleasure in experimentation was constant. Eclecticism was the key to his creativity.

292 The designer inside his studio with his dog, Harry. The furnishings of his atelier are equally dedicated to fusion, with a fascinating ensemble of old and new, industrial and exotic.

293 A play of volumes in the 2012 Spring/ Summer collection exhibited in Paris: the white bomber jacket serves as a counterpoint to the full circle of the black mermaid dress.

294 The masculine shirt—worn untucked—is set against the precious and opulent crystal-and-pearl encrustation of the coat, a typical feature of the Belgian designer, which also appeared in the 2013-2014 Fall/Winter collection.

"I'm known for color and prints and embroideries. Normally the more they clash, the more I like them." Textiles, processes, and colors thus arrived from around the world, with a predilection for the Middle and the Far East. Emanating from his creations were hints of India and China, subtle touches of Japan, and vibrant emotions from Bali, but, also, the strong heartbeat of Africa, and the intense passions of Persia. His style, however, was not banal or simplistically ethnic, as was so much other fashion in the 1990s. Rather, his power bordered upon a dialogue, and a contagion of diverse inspirations and impressions. In sum, exoticism, but one totally different from that which might be found on a postcard.

If the overused expression *mix and match*—the magic mantra of contemporary fashion—were to be attached to any designer, it would have to be Van Noten. His approach is contemporary, fresh, and unusual. He looks to old and new art, tossing elements from both into the cauldron of his imagination. His collections thus succeed in being simultaneously bohemian and sporty, eccentric and minimal, cerebral and sensual, posh and easy to sell.

"I am a little naïve, but I don't like the idea of showing things that you can't sell in a store." Sales revenues speak for him. His attendance at Jesuit schools impressed on him a work ethic that can be summarized as 'little pretense, much substance.' Nevertheless, many luxury stores throughout the world sell his collections, and the most sophisticated and unconventional of stars choose to wear his creations, on the most prestigious of occasions.

Actresses such as brand aficionado Maggie Gyllenhaal, or Cate Blanchett, who wore Van Noten at the most frequently photographed red-carpet occasion—the Oscars—in 2008, or Jane Birkin, who, subverting all unwritten rules, strutted down the red carpet in a knee-length, mustard-colored skirt and a caramel-colored, long woolen sweater. Van Noten does not chase the market; he does not design pre-collections; he does not put his signature on capsule collections, he does not engage in collaborations. "Personally, I think there is too much fashion in the world," he declares, and certainly not for the sake of provocation. He simply dedicates himself—with a self-denial bordering on rigidity—to his four annual collections, different, yet comparable, each time, as is the case with only the greatest figures in fashion. The rest of the time he can be found at home, immersed in greenery, a few kilometers from Antwerp, far from the smart set—intent on watering his roses and driving his little tractor. Of which he seems so proud.

296 Theatrical spiral maxi ruffles are the decorative leitmotif of the 2014 Spring/ Summer collection. We see them blossoming on tops, jackets, even skirts.

297 A dialogue among various, obviously incompatible prints in the 2012 Spring/ Summer collection: reproductions of antique lithographs of rural scenes in black and white, on the one hand, and details of blooming cherry-blossom set against a blue sky, on the other.

298 Flowers, tartan, and optical geometric patterns: a perfectly calibrated outfit by the designer, presented on the 2013 Spring/Summer collection runway that reaffirmed his status as master of the impossible combination.

299 Prints alluding to the Far East and disclosing the designer's love for the textiles and decorative culture of distant civilizations, evident and always passionate from the very outset.

AUTHOR

MARIA LUISA TAGARIELLO, earned a degree in Foreign Languages and Literature at the University of Bologna, then became a fashion journalist and copywriter. She was editor of >bmm, an independent art, fashion and design periodical, and collaborates with *style.it* and *vanityfair.it*, Condé Nast Italia online magazines. The author of books on shopping in the main fashion capitals, she has written a guidebook of London for the "Clup" series published by De Agostini. She now divides her time between fashion as a blogger and as editor of an online luxury boutique.

Guillaume Horcajuelo/epa/Corbis: page 173

Horst P. Horst/Condé Nast Archive/ Corbis: pages 25, 36

Frédéric Huijbregts/Corbis: page 55

Hulton Archive/Moviepix/Getty Images: page 68

Interfoto: page 134

Deutsch Jean-Claude/Paris Match/ Getty Images: page 133

Sauer Jean-Claude/Paris Match Archive/Getty Images: page 140

Kammerman/Gamma-Rapho/Getty Images: page 46

Douglas Kirkland/Corbis: page 69

Patrick Kovarik/AFP/Getty Images: pages 111, 112, 175

Josep Lago/AFP/Getty Images: page 62

Lancaster/Hulton-Deutsch Collection/ Corbis: page132

Pascal Le Segretain/Getty Images: page 218

Nina Leen/Time & Life Pictures/Getty Images: page 22

David Lees/Time & Life Pictures/Getty Images: pages 50, 52, 116

Elizabeth Lippman/The New York T/ Contrasto: page 145

Daniels Marleen/Hollandse Hoogte/ Contrasto: page 292

Jarnoux Maurice/Paris Match Archive/ Getty Images: page 67

MCT/McClatchy-Tribune/Getty Images: page 15 right

Miller/Interfoto: page 79

John Minihan/Hulton Archive/Getty Images: page 59

Mondadori Portfolio/Getty Images: page 177

Filippo Monteforte/AFP/Getty Images: pages 185, 205

David Montgomery/Hulton Archive/ Getty Images: page 153

Chris Moore/Catwalking/Getty Images: pages 167, 239, 273

Paul MorigiWireImage/Getty Images: page 147

Mudrats Alexandra/Photoshot/ Olycom: page 63

Jean-Pierre Muller/AFP/Getty Images: page 284

Terry O' Neill/Getty Images: page 151

Denis O'Regan/Hulton Archive/Getty Images: page 154

Anton Oparin/Shutterstock: page 6

Thierry Orban/Sygma/Corbis: page 104

Tony Palmieri/Condé Nast Archive/ Corbis: page 88

Gordon Parks/Time & Life Pictures/ Getty Images: page 31

Federico Patellani/Studio Patellani/ Corbis: page 78

Slade Paul/Paris Match Archive/Getty Images: pages 102, 103

Paolo Pellegrin/Contrasto: page 115

Jean-Marie Périer/Photo12: pages 166, 223, 233, 234, 250, 259

Courtesy of the Philadelphia Museum of Art: page 26

Philadelphia Museum of Art/Corbis: page 27

Photoshot/Olycom: page 215

Picture Alliance/Photoshot/Olycom: page 256

Karl Prouse/Catwalking/Getty Images: pages 120, 121, 149, 224, 227, 228, 229

Steve Pyke/Contour/Getty Images: page 281

Steve Pyke/Premium Archive/Getty Images: page 211

John Rawlings/Condé Nast Archive/ Corbis: page 70

Bill Ray/Time & Life Pictures/Getty Images: page 60

Retna/Photoshot/Olycom: pages 122-123, 156 right, 156 left, 219, 221, 237, 240, 241, 244, 245, 264, 266, 294, 296, 297

Willy Rizzo/Paris Match Archive/Getty Images: page 72

Alexis Rodriguez-Duarte/Corbis: page 187

Canio Romaniello/Olycom: pages 190, 193

Xavier Rossi/Gamma-Rapho/Getty Images: page 164

Rue des Archives/Archivi Farabola: page 214 right

Roger Schall/Condé Nast Archive/ Corbis: page 12

Ferdinando Scianna/Contrasto: pages 189, 192

Ferdinando Scianna/Magnum Photos/ Contrasto: pages 49, 134-135

Christophe Simon/AFP/Getty Images: page 203

Daniel Simon/Gamma-Rapho/Getty Images: pages 74, 91, 155

Pool Simon/Stevens/Gamma-Rapho: page 141

Snowdon/Camera Press/Contrasto: page 260

Kristy Sparow/Getty Images: page 171

Bert Stern/Condé Nast Archive/ Corbis: page 5

Richard Stonehouse/Camera Press/ Contrasto: page 194

Toni Thorimbert/Sygma/Corbis: page 188

UPPA/Photoshot/Olycom: page 17

Laurent Van der Stockt/Gamma-Rapho/Getty Images: pages 165, 248, 249

Pierre Vauthey/Sygma/Corbis: page 182

Venturelli/WireImage/Getty Images: page 98

Pierre Verdy/AFP/Getty Images: page 119

Laszlo Veres/Photo B.D.V./Corbis: pages 191, 195

Rinaldo Veronelli/Splash News/ Corbis: page 242

Victor Virgile/Gamma-Rapho: pages 274, 298, 299

Victor Virgile/Gamma-Rapho/Getty Images: pages 170, 174, 184, 206, 235, 243, 265, 269, 279

Sabine Weiss/Gamma-Rapho/Getty Images: page 131

Xinhua/Eyevine/Contrasto: pages 275, 277

Xinhua/Gamma-Rapho: pages 160, 276

Xinhua/Photoshot/Olycom: page 268

Naomi Yang/Figarophoto/Contour Style/Getty Images: page 201

Vittorio Zunino Celotto/Getty Images: page 117

Cover

A Mikado sculpted dress in 84 different colors by Roberto Capucci (2001).
© *Fiorenzo Niccoli/Archivio Giorgini Firenze*

Back cover

A portrait of Coco Chanel by the illustrator Junie Bro-Jorgensen (USA - 2009).
© *McClatchy-Tribune/Getty Images*

The Publisher would like to thank the Fondazione Roberto Capucci and the Fondazione Gianfranco Ferré.

NOTEN Coco CHANEL Elsa SCHIAPARELLI Cristóbal BALENCIAGA
Christian DIOR Emilio PUCCI Pierre CARDIN Hubert de GIVENCHY
Roberto CAPUCCI VALENTINO Karl LAGERFELD Giorgio ARMANI
Yves Saint LAURENT Ralph LAUREN Vivienne WESTWOOD Yohji
YAMAMOTO Gianfranco FERRÉ Gianni VERSACE Miuccia PRADA
Jean Paul GAULTIER Martin MARGIELA DOLCE & GABBANA John
GALLIANO Tom FORD Marc JACOBS Alexander McQUEEN Dries Van
NOTEN Coco CHANEL Elsa SCHIAPARELLI Cristóbal BALENCIAGA
Christian DIOR Emilio PUCCI Pierre CARDIN Hubert de GIVENCHY
Roberto CAPUCCI VALENTINO Karl LAGERFELD Giorgio ARMANI
Yves Saint LAURENT Ralph LAUREN Vivienne WESTWOOD Yohji
YAMAMOTO Gianfranco FERRÉ Gianni VERSACE Miuccia PRADA
Jean Paul GAULTIER Martin MARGIELA DOLCE & GABBANA John
GALLIANO Tom FORD Marc JACOBS Alexander McQUEEN Dries Van
NOTEN Coco CHANEL Elsa SCHIAPARELLI Cristóbal BALENCIAGA
Christian DIOR Emilio PUCCI Pierre CARDIN Hubert de GIVENCHY
Roberto CAPUCCI VALENTINO Karl LAGERFELD Giorgio ARMANI
Yves Saint LAURENT Ralph LAUREN Vivienne WESTWOOD Yohji
YAMAMOTO Gianfranco FERRÉ Gianni VERSACE Miuccia PRADA
Jean Paul GAULTIER Martin MARGIELA DOLCE & GABBANA John
GALLIANO Tom FORD Marc JACOBS Alexander McQUEEN Dries Van
NOTEN Coco CHANEL Elsa SCHIAPARELLI Cristóbal BALENCIAGA
Christian DIOR Emilio PUCCI Pierre CARDIN Hubert de GIVENCHY
Roberto CAPUCCI VALENTINO Karl LAGERFELD Giorgio ARMANI
Yves Saint LAURENT Ralph LAUREN Vivienne WESTWOOD Yohji

YAMAMOTO Gianfranco FERRÉ Gianni VERSACE Miuccia PRADA
Jean-Paul GAULTIER Martin MARGIELA DOLCE & GABBANA John
GALLIANO Tom FORD Marc JACOBS Alexander McQUEEN Dries VAN
NOTEN Coco CHANEL Elsa SCHIAPARELLI Cristóbal BALENCIAGA
Christian DIOR Emilio PUCCI Pierre CARDIN Hubert de GIVENCHY
Roberto CAPUCCI VALENTINO Karl LAGERFELD Giorgio ARMANI
Yves SAINT LAURENT Ralph LAUREN Vivienne WESTWOOD Yohji
YAMAMOTO Gianfranco FERRÉ Gianni VERSACE Miuccia PRADA
Jean-Paul GAULTIER Martin MARGIELA DOLCE & GABBANA John
GALLIANO Tom FORD Marc JACOBS Alexander McQUEEN Dries VAN
NOTEN Coco CHANEL Elsa SCHIAPARELLI Cristóbal BALENCIAGA
Christian DIOR Emilio PUCCI Pierre CARDIN Hubert de GIVENCHY
Roberto CAPUCCI VALENTINO Karl LAGERFELD Giorgio ARMANI
Yves SAINT LAURENT Ralph LAUREN Vivienne WESTWOOD Yohji
YAMAMOTO Gianfranco FERRÉ Gianni VERSACE Miuccia PRADA
Jean-Paul GAULTIER Martin MARGIELA DOLCE & GABBANA John
GALLIANO Tom FORD Marc JACOBS Alexander McQUEEN Dries VAN
NOTEN Coco CHANEL Elsa SCHIAPARELLI Cristóbal BALENCIAGA
Christian DIOR Emilio PUCCI Pierre CARDIN Hubert de GIVENCHY
Roberto CAPUCCI VALENTINO Karl LAGERFELD Giorgio ARMANI
Yves SAINT LAURENT Ralph LAUREN Vivienne WESTWOOD Yohji
YAMAMOTO Gianfranco FERRÉ Gianni VERSACE Miuccia PRADA
Jean-Paul GAULTIER Martin MARGIELA DOLCE & GABBANA John
GALLIANO Tom FORD Marc JACOBS Alexander McQUEEN Dries VAN
NOTEN Coco CHANEL Elsa SCHIAPARELLI Cristóbal BALENCIAGA